Weird in a World That's Not

Weird in a World That's Not

A Career Guide for Misfits, F*ckups, and Failures

Jennifer Romolini

HARPER
BUSINESS

An Imprint of HarperCollins*Publishers*

I have changed the names of some individuals and modified identifying features, such as physical descriptions and occupations, of other individuals in order to preserve their anonymity. In some cases, composite characters have been created, or timelines have been compressed, in order to further preserve privacy and to maintain narrative flow. The goal in all cases was to protect people's privacy without damaging the integrity of the story.

FIRST EDITION

Library of Congress Cataloging-in-Publication Data has been applied for.

ISBN 978-0-06-247272-4

17 18 19 20 21   LSC   10 9 8 7 6 5 4 3 2 1

For Lynn and for Charlotte

and for weird girls everywhere

Contents

Part I: Find Your Weird

Part II: Embrace Your Weird

Part III: Weird in the World

Prologue

ere are my worst fears. You should probably know them, since we're about to spend a lot of time together.

I am afraid of home invasions, even though it's been explained to me statistically that they make up around 0.000015 percent of all robberies and that for every horrifying "evil humans broke in, stole everything, and all the house dwellers were mutilated except the dad who had to watch" there are thousands of seconds-long laptop-and-jewels snatch jobs where no one is hurt, not even the dog. The actual odds of a home invasion happening to me are less than the odds that I have the Zika virus. Still, when I lived alone in Brooklyn, I pushed my dresser in front of my bedroom door every night before bed. Still, I look up "do I have Zika" more than I should.

I have a garden-variety fear of dying before age ninety-seven, which I suspect is less about actual death than about how much, despite my incessant bitching, I am obsessed with being alive (there are never enough years in a world that has both alcohol and kittens. I imagine you understand). I crave the opportunity to grow old, to exclusively wear caftans, to play an accordion on a front porch while drinking whiskey, to freak out the neighborhood kids just because I'm still here. I fear I will not get this.

I am afraid of heights. I discovered this fear not in the summers I spent jumping off rural-Pennsylvania cliffs into rural-Pennsylvania creeks to impress rural-Pennsylvania boys, but instead in my early thirties, at a "corporate offsite," a mandatory adult field trip I had to attend for a new job. I had just landed a position working for an Internet company with an office based in New York City, where I lived. I was hired to write about fashion and beauty *on the Internet, from my home,* but somehow, as part of my employment agreement, I had to fly to Los Angeles, take a bus to Malibu, to a farm where they once filmed an *America's Next Top Model* challenge, and climb a rope obstacle course with people I did not know. This was so we could prove that we could work together, even though we'd never really have to work together.

Upon arrival, after niceties and name tags, I was assigned a team, fitted with a helmet and a groin holster, and asked to ascend a two-story rope ladder. According to the ropes-course website, this activity would bolster my self-esteem and teach me how to trust. According to the website, the entire day would build personal development, teamwork, and accountability, and help me glean critical skills for on-the-job life. It was a day of next-level trust falls, with the addition of a waiver you had to sign in case you died.

There were several obstacle courses at our ropes camp, but the goal of the one I'd been assigned, the "high" version, was to climb to the top of the rope ladder, swing myself over to an adjacent pole, and then climb that, just like an old-timey telephone-line repair person would. After reaching the highest rung, I was then supposed to hoist myself onto a plate—which was nailed down in the middle of the pole and resembled an upside-down Frisbee—balance upon the wobbly Frisbee plate, and then, with a rope attached to my groin holster, float like a graceful winged fairy to the ground.

I tried and failed three times to climb to the top of the rope course that day, each attempt longer, sweatier, and more panicked, my new teammates cheering me on—"You can do it!"—and the coach shouting "How bad do you want this?" and "How can we help Jennifer succeed?" I did not in fact want it, and I could not in fact do it, and because my body had already betrayed me, because it'd frozen at the top in a kind of arms-bent doll pose, as if my joints were decorative or I needed a Tin Man oiling, my team could not in fact help me succeed. From my perch I could see all of Malibu, a place I'd never been before, all mountains, treetops, and mansions; all butterflies, golden light, and wealth. From my perch I imagined falling, a scene with an ambulance and EMTs, rope too tight around my waist to be untied, dramatically cut from my body as they wheeled me off on a gurney, a slow-wave good-bye from my teammates who were watching from the sidelines. I wondered what the fancy-rich-people Malibu hospital would be like inside.

I balanced motionless, mute, helmet-clad, and grimacing

like this way for too long, until it got weird and was not fun anymore, until there was *concern* from the people in charge. Finally some capable person decided to climb up and help me. We sailed down, conjoined in a vertical spooning position, my arms still Barbie-bent against my sides, uncomfortable feelings and stares all around.

After the ropes course, our team was asked to create an actual cheerleader-like cheer about why we loved the company more than anyone else loved the company and then perform the cheer in front of all the other groups. The group who won was awarded a prize that I don't remember because it was not my group that won. Turns out I am also afraid of performing company-propaganda cheers in front of dozens of strangers.

Rounding out the team-building day, employees gathered to eat soggy sandwiches in a tented makeshift cafeteria and watch a "sizzle reel" of company highlights set to very excited stock music. It was an absurd situation, one made even more so because the people around me seemed to be having a good time—they were *into it* and *having fun*. I felt out of place, awkward and exposed, a Woman Who Fell to Earth If Earth Was a Contrived Corporate Retreat.

By the end of the day, I was sure I would never make it at that job. Instead I stayed there for six years, was promoted four times, and earned more money than I'd ever imagined I would. I succeeded in that job and in even bigger jobs after it. I became great at what I did, growing into the kind of effective, powerful #boss human I'd admired but did not imagine I could be. I choked that day at the ropes course, and I kept choking, but I made it despite myself.

Which leads me to the biggest, most sustained fear of my life, one that I've only recently overcome: for a long time, I was pretty sure I would never make it in the world, that I would never become "successful," in the way that successful people are. The reason I would never do this was because I was too intense, too socially clumsy, too *sensitive* to ever hold down a J-O-B, to ever be a "professional" on the terms of the professional world. I worried that people like me just didn't get to make it. I could not see the way into my dream life, and for a long time, up until my mid-twenties, I could not even bring myself to identify what those dreams could be.

As I began a search for my "calling" and as I moved into my career, there were questions I desperately needed answered. Things like: How do I make an intellectual class jump without leaving my working-class family behind? How do I navigate awkward networking without getting sloppy drunk to hide my nerves? How do I survive intense office politics? When will I start to feel like I actually belong? How (and when) do I leave a shitty job? How can I be a truly great boss when managing is the worst, when everyone wants to take advantage of you/make you solve their problems/steal your soul? How do I walk the line between being ambitious, competitive, and powerful and being a 1980s-movie dragon career lady in shoulder-pads who everyone hates (and I hate too)? And, most important: How do I do all this and stay true to who I am?

But in all the successful-habits-parachutes-tips-boss-cheese-

moving-life-goals-inspiration-boards books I read, I found no
answers. And I could not find a model for someone like me: a
mere mortal who spent too much on condiments, spaced out
at the mention of a 401(k), frittered away hours of life stalking
exes on social media, and sniffing clothes before putting them
on in the morning. Don't get me wrong: I love, respect, and admire the people who wrote all those career books. I appreciate
their confidence, their experience, and the fact that their pants
are not stained. I'm just not like them.

And no one ever told me there was another way, that outliers like me were allowed to succeed in conventional business.
We've provided few models for successful misfits on conference panels or in conference rooms. Either you are a Business
Man or Business Lady, a stoic, contained person with perfect
hair, smiling confidently but without too many teeth showing,
or you are a basket case who needs to be dragged off by security. Culture tells us that true misfits are only allowed in artsy,
fringe careers; allowed to write our poetry, bake our artisanal
cupcakes, open our Etsy shops, and loom our hand-loomed vagina pillows. They pat us on our heads and talk about our left
brains. They say that we're too emotional to be lawyers, we can't
be businesspeople because we're too odd. But they are wrong.

Being a weirdo or an outlier or even a slacker and achieving
real, high-level success are not mutually exclusive, even if all
the CEOs you've seen look vanilla and the same. And even if
all the business-success books are written by normals who you
couldn't imagine struggling with e-mail hoarding and having
toothpaste in their hair. You are not shut out of the club just

because you are awkward and not perfect or don't look the part. Perfection is a fantasy anyway. If you are a card-carrying weirdo, your sensitivity and raw way of being in the world is not a detriment, it's an asset. Your all-in, all-fucks-given intensity, your *difference*, is exactly what makes you special and a breath of fresh air in the business world. Your weirdness is an asset. Embracing it (in addition to working hard and becoming great at what you do) will help you succeed in almost any profession that you feel passionate about. If you want it, you can have a totally rewarding career that makes you real money *and* allows you to stay true to the misfit you really are.

You're just going have to overcome some bullshit first.

This is a career book for people like me. It's a guide for the awkward, the misfits, the fuckups, and the failures. This is a book about finding your inner tenacity and path, about wanting it and making it happen while remaining true to yourself—even (and especially) if you're weird and the odds seem stacked against you.

How to Use This Book

You should use this book however you want! Stop pressuring yourself! Shut off your type-W brain and jump ahead to what is most relevant to your experience right now—be it interviewing or resigning or dealing with haters or managing. If you don't want to hear me blather on about myself, if you need support rightthissecond, skip ahead to the ADVICE (specifically to page 47). Use this book as a reference over the next few years of your career, pick it up and put it down when you need help, when you feel lost, use it the way you did a puberty guide, skim it all at once, cross-check the table of contents for the juiciest parts, and then read VERY CLOSELY when a specific situation is happening to you.

The only rule of this book is that you be kind to yourself while you're reading it, that you know that it's all going to be OK and you are fine. This book is not meant to transform you into something you are not; it's here to support you and help you be successful by remaining or discovering exactly who you are.

Introduction

Why I'm Here

I am not supposed to be here. I spent the first twenty-eight years of my life as a fuckup and a failure. I failed and I failed and I failed. I failed out of college because I was too stoned to make it to class. I had a failed marriage before most people even start their first real relationship. I spent a decade wandering and failing, I wasted years of my young life lost and sad and mad and struggling and drunk. I failed at finances, I failed at jobs. I nearly didn't even graduate high school because I was failing gym.

Just a few years ago, I was not a person who could write a how-to-make-it-in-your-career memoir. Just a few years ago, I was sitting in a car, in the cold, in a driveway, alone on a winter's morning, trying to leave my first husband. I was twenty-four, I was a waitress and a college dropout, I had less than $100 in the bank. I was living in a small town in Pennsylvania, and I was deeply unhappy—the kind of unhappiness that drapes over you like a cloak, the kind of unhappiness you feel when you know you are living the wrong life and have no idea what to do about it.

The morning I tried to leave my husband happened after many mornings of wanting to leave my husband. We'd started out vibrant, young, and different—he was a Miata-driving, khakis-wearing nice guy who punctuated conversation with finger-guns, and I was a hyperemotional, arty girl in tank tops with no bras who knew how to have fun—but now we were strange broken shells of people with little in common except a license to stay together and a stubborn need to save face in front of everyone who said it would fail. We'd lost each other early on, with a baby who was supposed to come but never came (at 4.5 months, a week before our wedding, my body failed at pregnancy)—a loss more devastating than our dumb-young, not-fully-formed brains could bear. Now we lied to each other to get through the day, drank too much at night, and fought so loudly from our ground-floor apartment that the neighbors regularly complained.

The morning that I tried to leave my husband came after I'd waited up for him all night, just like I'd waited up for him loads of nights; pacing the apartment, flipping the TV on and off, paging through magazines, holding our weird-sad overweight cat. Something was happening to me, something full and deep and unexplainable, something I didn't want to think about too much for fear it would go away. In my mind, I was getting ready to go, to accept the possibility that there was more, that I could be more, that I could exist outside what I'd known.

I'd married too young, without thought for my independence, my identity, or especially my future. I married because I thought I should, because it seemed presumptuous and even pretentious to have highfalutin dreams of professional success, and even more impossible to make those dreams come true. I married at twenty-one because I genuinely thought I was too messed up to go it alone, and because I thought a man could save me.

At 4:00 a.m., I packed a bag. I wrote a speech. I practiced the speech. And I waited. The windows were fogged in our apartment complex, but my mind was clear. This would be my last night in this life. The sun came up over the snowy windowsills. I heard my husband's car pull into the driveway. He stumbled inside; I sputtered out my speech. I picked up my bag, walked out, and shut the door behind me. Then I got into my car, backed it up, and . . . my car broke down in the driveway.

There are a few defining moments in every person's life, and that morning in the cold, staring back at a home and a life that I knew was not meant for me, was one of mine. Watching my husband peek intermittently through the curtain, knowing I had to go back inside, I realized I really had nothing. I had zero prospects. I had no money, no education, no career path, and no real marketable skills. I was in my mid-twenties, and I was not only directionless but entirely dependent on a man. I vowed in that moment that it would never happen again.

I vowed in that moment to get control of my life and to change my destiny, and that's just what I did.

It didn't all happen that day. I didn't fix my car and suddenly drive off into some success sunset. It would take years to dig out and catch up and build the professional and personal life I wanted. It would take sacrifices and positive thinking and luck and tenacity and moments when I was terrified and work was the only thing that mattered—and it would take climbing, lots of climbing, because the only way out of a hole is to crawl-climb your way up.

Why You're Here

You're here because you've spent a good part of your life feeling different and outside. You're here because you've been told that you "think too much" or you're "so intense" or your sensitivity is a sign of weakness. Because you don't actually feel like a badass, and no matter how many TED talks you watch on personal power and Wonder Woman posing, the experience of being at work often makes you feel anxious and strange. You want a map for how to be a professional—but as yourself, preserving who you are; staying open and honest, maintaining connection to your inner freak. You are here because you are looking for the secret codes for how to navigate all of this. And you want them told to you in a way that makes practical sense, that doesn't make you feel like you need to change your fundamental being to perform well in an interview or give a PowerPoint presentation. So much of our careers feels like banging on doors to see which one will let us in, feeling in the dark to find the next rung on the ladder or jungle gym or whatever we're calling it. And it's easy to get lost in this. You're looking for a guide.

You're here because you're just starting out, trying to find your first job or what it is you actually want to do. Or you're somewhere in the middle of your career and you've hit a wall, you're stuck and you're thinking, "How the *hell* do I get out of this?" "Is this all there is?" "What is my next move?" Or maybe you're lost, feeling like you've fucked everything up, taken a wrong turn. You're tired of insurance sales; your soul wants to design dresses, but you're too afraid to try.

No matter which of these stages of your professional life you're in today, you're here because you don't just want a job, you want a fulfilling career (at least one—you'll probably have several). You want to be challenged, inspired, ultimately more successful, and better compensated than you are today. You will spend 90,000 hours of your life working. That's more than you will spend doing anything else except sleeping. And you know you owe it to yourself to make those hours the most meaningful that they can possibly be. You know you can't resign yourself to a listless job. You don't want to spend your one life grinding out work you care little about, a sad office-humor cliché.

You're here because you want more out of your career, even

as you're facing a stupid-tight and ever-shifting job market, nagging self-doubt, the challenges of rampant sexism and racism in the workplace, a persistent wage gap (particularly for women of color), a lack of precedent for female leadership in most careers, a lack of mentors, and mansplaining men everywhere you look.

You're here because you're tired of feeling quite so delicate, one professional rejection away from emotional cataclysm, a floor puddle of Chunky Monkey and Netflix. Because you want to get stronger and more sure-footed. Because you don't want to be tripped up by small things like what to say in an e-mail, and big ones like how to ask for a raise. Because you don't yet know when you need to stand up for yourself and when you definitely *don't* need to stand up for yourself. You're here because you haven't realized yet that you're not alone, that even your heroes think they are impostors, that we all think we don't deserve to be here, we all believe, despite overwhelming evidence to the contrary, that we are irrelevant, incompetent trash people, and soon THEY ARE ALL GOING TO KNOW.

You are here because no matter how nasty the self-talk and shitty programming that's intermittently popping off in your brain, the voices that tell you you're lazy, untalented, the worst, you need to find empathy for yourself, you need someone to tell you how you are feeling is normal. That you belong. That you CAN do this.

Because you can.

No matter where you are today, no how matter how you're feeling about yourself, this book is here to retrain your brain, to teach you a new message: You actually can do anything. You can reinvent yourself. You can find your life's purpose, find quality mentors in your profession; you can create a plan, and you can make that plan happen. Your up-until-this-point failures and self-doubt mean nothing unless you let them stand in your way. You can survive any wrong turns. You can learn how to feel normal at work and achieve anything you want. You can make it. No matter how weird or messed up you feel, you can soar.

PART I

Find Your
Weird

CHAPTER 1

Kooks

It's hard to pinpoint a precise start date for my weirdness. It is, as most things in life, inextricably linked to my parents—their successes and failures; their choices and fate. In order to share my story, I need to share theirs, at least for context.

My mom was sixteen when she met my dad. She was skinny and tall, a second-generation Italian American girl with angular features and dark hair nearly to her waist. She wore baby-doll dresses over bell-bottom dungarees and was tough, smart, and young-Cher pretty. She was poor, living at the time with her mother, my grandmother, a struggling single mom. My grandfather was an opera singer but mostly a grifter, mostly a cheat. When he left, my grandmother experienced severe bouts of depression that sometimes led her to severe situations involving straitjackets and electric shock treatments and, finally, lots and lots of Catholic God. My mom was the only one around to deal.

When my parents met, my dad was a seventeen-year-old high-school dropout hauling around a set of torment baggage perhaps even heavier than my mom's. He was a runaway and a bit of a thug, hanging on corners at night and during the day, working at a deli in the southwest section of Philly, where they sold cigarettes, which my mother came in and bought. My parents started dating. They went to see *Play Misty for Me*. Their song was Roberta Flack's "The First Time Ever I Saw Your Face." They escaped into each other and fell deeply in love. A year later I was born. A few months earlier, at their wedding in my grandmother's living room, my dad wore the same suit he had worn to take my mom to the prom.

We lived in a rickety row house on a run-down block in a poor part of Philadelphia next to a dive bar called Tex's Tavern. My parents fixed up the house with spider ferns and macramé and a blue shag carpet, and at some point we got a dinged-up white piano, though no one could play. We had a dog named Puppy for a time and an aquarium with a wide-eyed catfish who grew to be bigger than my arm. We had an iguana named Nighta whom we fed bananas until he died one day behind the couch. We had a turntable stored in a cinderblock shelving system my dad built where we played Led Zeppelin, Pink Floyd, and Jethro Tull albums on repeat, and a round dining room table that was rarely not strewn with ashtrays and wicker-wrapped Italian wine.

Teenagers are impetuous and passionate. Teenagers' brains are not fully formed. My parents were no different. My parents and their friends lived a teenage-appropriate life: they drank too many things, they smoked too many things; they had impromptu dance parties and inappropriate jealousies. They made terrible impulsive decisions and wonderful impulsive ones too. Our 1970s life was extreme—extremely happy, extremely sad, and sometimes extremely violent. My parents tried new drugs and new diets and new politics and then, when they grew tired of these things, went on spontaneous road trips with their friends. I went on these road trips too. I was the only kid around.

We shared motel rooms at the beach, we shared cabins in the mountains. Women wore caftans and men brought flutes and bongos, guitars and weed. When we got home, I played in a fort we'd made out of a cardboard refrigerator box. At night, in bed, I pulled the covers over my head and staged my stuffed animals in a pile over them, disguising the lump of my body so no one would know I was there.

On Sundays my parents and I got dressed up and drove deep into South Philadelphia to my great-grandfather's house for family dinners. He was an off-the-boat Italian, red horn in the doorway of his row home, red tomatoes growing in buckets in his cement backyard. Downstairs, in the basement, he made fresh linguine, pizza, and barrels of red wine. He sculpted birds out of iron. He played the violin. The house smelled of flour and disinfectant and dried peppers. He spoke broken Italian and broken English with a thick Old World accent. He called me Jen-o-eff and Jen-o-fee. He was an orphan who came to America after World War I. No one really hired Italians back then, they said; he'd never really had a job. My great-grandmother had supported the family as a seamstress, but that was before. Now she sat in a wheelchair in the corner of the room, by the window, overlooking the narrow South Philly street where they lived. She called me "Mommy"; she gave me quarters and folded-up dollar bills. She asked me to pick up thread and crumbs and fuzz she saw but couldn't lift from the ground.

There are stories I remember from these years and stories

I don't. They are told today around big tables in the suburbs where my parents and their friends catch up and talk and where I am treated like I am the child of all of them. Some of the stories are mild, and some are cool: I met David Bowie when I was just over a year old. My mom was a Bowie super fan; the song "Kooks," about a baby born to two free-spirited misfits (Bowie and his wife, presumably), was a kind of family anthem. My mom had seen Bowie in concert several times but was desperate to meet him. At a show one night in the city she and I waited outside the back entrance of the stadium for hours. When Bowie finally emerged, he paused at my mom. He stopped and signed her album. He touched my face and said I was cute. Everyone was excited, everyone was delighted.

There are other stories too, like the one where we're all on a summer road trip in rural New Jersey, driving in separate cars. My mom and I and some friends are in a van, and my dad and his friends are driving in another car, and somehow in the bustle of stopping at a rest stop, unloading, and getting back in the cars, I'm left behind as everyone drives off. They realized their mistake a few miles up the road, I'm told, shouting at each other, at high speed, through open windows: "Do you have Jennifer?" "No, do you?"

When my parents returned, they found me off to the side, sitting under a tree. I had been there less than a half hour, but even now, I imagine it as a full day.* I was four.

Who knows how we become people, how we map our patterns of joy and loss and failure into one walking-around-the-planet human. Who knows whether I understood loneliness

---

* My mother says it was five minutes.

for the first time that day or whether I understood it through the hundreds of subtle around-people-but-inside-yourself seconds that happen throughout a life, all lives, seconds the hypersensitive can rarely escape. But I know this: that day at the rest stop is one of my first vivid memories of being alive. I have felt other, like an outsider looking in, since.

Sometime after the rest-stop day, we all started to grow up. My parents, now in their early twenties, buckled down and started becoming more adult—my sister was born, they now had two kids to feed. My dad, who was always smart and resourceful, became more so, leveraging his position in the stock room at the local grocery store into viable self-employment and beginning to build a business that would eventually get us up and out of poverty and into a comfortable middle-class life. My mother worked too—in a department store in a posh part of Philly as a makeup counter girl, later as a hairdresser. Once my dad started his business, she took over the accounting, staying up late every night, counting and wrapping stacks of bills and rolling change into neat circular sleeves, tapping away at her bookkeeper's calculator while sitting cross-legged on our living room floor. I could hear the numbers clicking long into the night.

My dad started every workday at 3:00 a.m. He drove his beat-up Chevy Nova to Philadelphia's blocks-long Wholesale Produce Market because that was the time when you got the best stuff. My mother stayed up every night, after nursing and cooking for and feeding and bathing two kids, cleaning and washing and folding and putting away everyone's clothes, to pay bills, to balance profits and losses. She couldn't make mistakes; there was too much at stake. She was twenty-two. My parents were high-school dropouts with no education and just a great deal of common sense and tenacity; they created professional lives out of nothing. If there is any secret to my success, it is them. I learned more from watching them work hard than I did in all my (many) years of school.

Friends Don't Let Friends Get Perms

When do we start to understand that we're different? How do we know we're weird? For me, it began when I was nine. We'd moved to the suburbs, to an old farmhouse on an acre of land, some of it wooded. We were city folk in what felt like the country. My sister and I climbed trees and picked flowers from the honeysuckle bushes and ran through neighbors' yards and tried to make friends and tried to fit in. My brilliant, forever-attention-grabby brother was born, diluting our family's parental resources and leaving less acute guidance to go around.

Around the same time, I got bad glasses and a bad perm. Then I got braces. The dorkdom trifecta. My best friend, Clayton (a fellow misfit who would go on to become one of the world's most beautiful men, but at the time was a chubby kid with a mullet), and I rode bikes around the neighborhood and called our enemies "blank heads" like the true toughs we were. I played with Barbies until I was thirteen. I nicknamed myself Rambo and tagged my name all over school property while wearing an oversize denim jacket adorned with suede cowgirl tassels and a pin that proclaimed, menacingly, "I love everybody and you're next!"

Neither focused enough to be a nerd nor brave enough to be

a rebel, I was unpopular at school and had a hard time making friends. I was a mediocre student with a mess of limbs I did not know what to do with—when we played dodgeball, I often would get hit so hard I had to be sent to the nurse. Sometimes, either from the stress of PE or the exertion, I just passed out. On my school picture from sixth grade, someone affixed the sticker "Turn out the lights!"

My mother chaperoned my seventh-grade class field trip wearing high-top red Reeboks and tight acid-wash jeans. I overheard a kid on the bus say, "Jenn's mom's cool, what happened to Jenn?" It wasn't just my mom. I was born into a family of beautiful Italian Americans with Italian American swag. They strutted around in leather jackets and drove sleek Cadillacs. They were brazen, charismatic, *Goodfellas* charming; they could talk to anyone in any room. I did not possess this same physical presence or confidence; I didn't really even understand where my body was in space. I was a sensitive, awkward over-thinker with zero chill; I never met a chair I could not manage to fall out of, a sidewalk I could not trip upon, a person waving at someone else at whom I would not mistakenly wave back. My Italian American cousins were slick, dark-haired clones of their parents—tough, loud, self-possessed. I was out of step with my cultural identity, and it showed.

But my foundational weirdness didn't end there. As my parents' partying days mellowed, as they grew less interested in intoxication and escape and more into *meaning*, we became a family of spiritual and emotional contradictions. At our core, we were aggressive working-class Catholic Italians, but we were journeying into a late-1980s New Age. Our house was filled with Marianne Williamson tapes, Shirley Maclaine books, incense, and aura-clearing crystals, but this somehow failed to stop us from regularly gritting our teeth in rage, screeching expletives, or chasing each other around the dining room table with plastic knives. At this time, my parents relied on the principles of reincarnation and positive affirmations the way some families leaned on after-work martinis or kitchen-cabinet Valium. They temporarily masked our problems, but didn't solve anything.

We blamed things on karma, we lit chakra candles, yet my mom would regularly get so angry with customer service reps that she'd scream into and bang the phone. My dad carried both a bat and a machete in his car "just in case." There was a general sense that "giving them a piece of my mind" was a good way to resolve conflict, but also that maybe someone's motivations came from a past life.

Perhaps as a response to all of this, or more likely, a response to puberty, I developed into an extra-moody, extra-maudlin kid. On summer days, while my father worked and my mother ran errands and everyone else was outside playing and sporting and hanging and being cool, I stayed inside, loosened my braces with a butter knife, and watched soap operas. I can essentially tell you all of the plot points from *The Young and the Restless*, *The Bold and the Beautiful*, and *As the World Turns* from the years 1983 to 1987. At night I watched reruns of *Dynasty*, *Falcon Crest*, *Dallas*, and *Knots Landing*. I was obsessed with rich people, middle-aged people, and dramatic, cosmopolitan stories of adulthood, different from the one around me.

My favorite films at this time were late-1970s and early-1980s movies you could catch at odd times on the Home Box Office channel, which I taped on VHS. My library included *Only*

When I Laugh (with Marsha Mason and Kristy McNichol, about an alcoholic theater actress and single mom trying to raise her daughter in Manhattan); *Kramer vs. Kramer* (with Dustin Hoffman and Meryl Streep, a story of divorce set in New York City), and *The Four Seasons* (with Alan Alda and Mary Tyler Moore; four middle-aged couples go away every season together until one couple divorces because of the man's midlife crisis). I watched these movies again and again. I cooked boxes of instant Stouffer's stuffing, ate it out of a pot, and whiled away hours on the couch. I was lazy. And I lived with industrious parents.

Starting at age thirteen, they put me to work.

Happy Holidays, Hon

Every Easter my dad—who now owned three fruit and vegetable markets around Philadelphia and southern New Jersey—would set up a flower stand outside his main store in Philly to attract customers, and because I had the week off for spring break, every Easter he brought me in to work it. On the first morning, he'd show me the inventory: pallets of bright flowers, hundreds of them, which would be moved around the back warehouse throughout the week by men driving forklifts. I liked the smell of the warehouse—pungent and rotting and earthy, like counter tomatoes bought hopefully and then gone bad, culinary hopes taken with them. I liked walking into the deep refrigerator, filled with bananas, peppers, and lettuces, with its heavy door and ribbons-of-plastic entrance, which looked like spaghetti or the long soapy snakes at the car wash. I liked the bustle of the men who worked for my father, their roughness and thick, vowel-ing Philly accents, how they listened to Howard Stern in the morning and classic rock in the afternoon and made dirty jokes all day (at least when they thought I wasn't around). I even liked the warehouse bathroom, filthy in a way that would never come clean, a kind of filth that suggested that this was a different land with different laws, with signs and slang on the walls that I did not understand.

After the big inventory reveal, my dad would explain each plant's wholesale and retail costs so I would know how much I could lower the prices while bargaining with customers and still turn a profit. If we turned a profit, he would split the revenue with me; if we didn't, he would take the loss. He didn't really care about making money from the flowers (which I understood to be a losing inventory anyway); he just wanted an attractive display and a friendly person outside to bring in foot traffic.

We started on Mondays—optimistic with dozens of perky, multihued potted tulips, hyacinths, azaleas, and lilies—and ended Saturday, unless things were really slow and we had a ton left to sell, when I came in for one last push on Easter Sunday morning to capture the after-church crowd. Depending on the heat and quality of that year's stock, the flowers usually started to wilt by Wednesday. By Thursday afternoon they were drooping in earnest, and by Saturday morning my stand was mostly an unholy mess, and I was propping limp buds up with Popsicle sticks just to make them appear alive. As my flowers became more obviously listless, some passersby laughed and some appeared concerned. The cantankerous complained. Still I made deals. I made funny signs. I offered buy-two-get-one-free specials. When married men said they could not bring half-dead flowers home to their wives, I suggested that they take the dormant tulips and plant them as a surprise—they were bulbs! They were perennials! They would come up next year! Sometimes I was outsmarted by old Italian ladies who would unburden me of a case or two; I'd agree to anything to get flowers out of our warehouse and more money into our pockets, only realizing when I checked the math that I'd been totally ripped off. Middle-aged moms would take pity on me, grab a pot of sad flowers on their way out, and hand over their $2 with a pat on my shoulder and a "Happy holidays, hon."

Some years I made $100; some years it was zero, but my dad would give me $50 anyway. One year I made $256 and spent it all on clothes and shoes for school. I can still feel the thrill of buying an oversize Garfield T-shirt with my own money.

In my last year, on a particularly grim, gray Easter morning, when I was about to close up shop, an Eastern European man in his late forties approached the stand. He said he'd been watching me all week and wanted to know my name. He'd also like to know my age. I told him I had to get my dad. I brought my dad outside, and the two men moved to the side and talked for a while as I packed up. When they were finished, the man shook my dad's hand, got back in his car, and drove off. Back inside the store, I asked my dad what had happened. He explained that the man was looking for a wife and wanted to know how much I would cost. He dragged the story out, as if he'd entertained the offer, as if he was thinking it over, and then gave me a look: "I would never." He hugged me tight. Those weeks selling flowers are some of the closest I've ever felt to my father. But I was getting too old for the job. After the Russian-bride incident, I retired.

But I never stopped working after that. I liked having my own money, liked the independence of existing in a universe that my parents did not control. My early work life, however, met with mixed success. For every after-school and weekend job I got, I was fired from two: I was fired from the Gap for refusing to wear socks with my Vans ("Gap people wear socks," I was told); from the Limited for not being encouraging enough to customers in the dressing rooms ("Tell everyone they look GREAT in the clothes!" "But what if they don't?"); from Bath & Body Works because I would not sit through a three-day orientation on fruit scents; from Bennigan's because I complained about having to shadow another server for a week before getting paid. I was let go from a telemarketing company that sold death and dismemberment insurance because I couldn't stay on script, and from a hostess job at a tapas restaurant chain because, even though, yes, I would wear the sequin vest and sing "Happy Birthday" in Spanish to rude Ivy League college boys, the boss was a total creep, and one night I just had to tell him to fuck off.

I did better at smaller, independently owned institutions with fewer oppressive and draconian rules. I sliced lunch meat and made cheesesteaks at a deli down the street from my high school, owned by an Italian American family who employed all of their sons and wanted a girl around. On Saturdays I would head directly there after the art class I took in the city, portfolio under my arm, and show my coworkers my drawings from that day. They didn't get what I was doing (I don't really know if I did either), but they treated me like I was arty and special and I loved them for it and worked hard for them, even ratting out kids my age who came in and tried to buy beer. I made pizzas and calzones and worked the phones at our local pizza place and sometimes made out with the delivery guy between orders. I solo-manned the video store counter at my best friend's dad's video store, where I loved recommending movies and also first discovered gay porn.

I liked working, I just had no idea what I liked to do. And toward the end of my time at my very large, very public high school, it was pretty clear that I had no idea what I *wanted* to do either. I was not heading to Harvard, or anywhere like Harvard. I'd failed various math and science classes so many times that by senior year I was enrolled in a basic geometry class where I swear we just drew shapes, and a class called Environmental Science, which involved me and a bunch of burnouts walking around the park behind school while they got stoned and I collected creek samples and worms (the only class that year in which I got an A). There were other problems too. My SAT score was a 910 out of 1600, with an even, below-average split between math and English. When I took the test a second time, the score was even worse. I was also failing gym—for being late, for forgetting my uniform, for not wanting to square-dance. I lacked the discipline, focus, and fear of authority that helps most kids succeed in high school; I wanted out of the social quagmire and away from arbitrary rules. Though it would take me years—decades—to recognize it, under all my identity decoration I was pissed off and hurting, somewhat from feeling odd and other, somewhat from issues at home (lingering alcoholism, marital discord, the attendant unpleasantness of both—this is another book). More than anything, however, even then, I craved a different life, one I could live on my own weird terms.

Upon learning of the gym situation, my mom sat me down and asked what I wanted to do. There were options, she said. I could drop out and learn a trade. I could be a hairdresser. I could drop out, get my GED, live at home, and try some community college courses while I sorted things out. Or I could buckle down and get my grades up to a C average, enough to graduate, accept the one state-school college admission I'd been offered, and go away in the fall with my friends.

I chose college. I chose getting out and going away. I did extra credit, I studied, I washed my uniform and played volleyball in gym. While my class enjoyed two days off before graduation, I spent them entirely in the dean's office to offset the hours I owed in detention. For the first time, I understood that last-ditch efforts actually can turn things around, that when you show people you want to get better, they actually want to help—and this wasn't some movie lie. For the first time, I realized that you're not necessarily as doomed as you think you are, even when you're up against a wall and it all seems hopeless, a revelation I've turned to in seemingly hundreds of situations since. I graduated with my class and went to college the following fall. I chose adventure and the unknown because I'd rather take a risk than stay in an old funk. Even though I basically failed college upon arrival, taking a leap into something new has been the only consistent pathway to success I've known in an otherwise long road of fucking up.

CHAPTER 2

School Daze

Here is a summation of my first three years in college: *Weed weed beer beer* art student boyfriend in a band *weed* 1.4 GPA *beer weed* identity crisis *weed* arrested *beer eight-foot bong beer* self-loathing *weed beer shots* heartbreak friend drama *weed weed* nervous breakdown *weed beer* cut off by parents *weed malt liquor weed* panic attack *beer weed* kicked out for good. And then I got knocked up.

You'll notice that there's nothing in here about actual school. That's because I did not go to actual school, at least not very often, and when I did, I did not do actual work, at least not enough to pass. Within less than three years, I would fail out of my slightly artsy, Amish country–adjacent, middle-of-nowhere Pennsylvania state school for good. In those three years, I had not one single class that made me feel inspired, not one academic experience that made me feel a sense of path or purpose or passion. But that doesn't mean I didn't learn anything, nor that the experiences I had over those three years didn't shape me in important ways. And it's important to note here that every single thing you do, including whatever it is you're doing right now (Are you lying on the floor watching *Friends* reruns? That counts.) will have meaning later on. You shouldn't dismiss any of your experiences as insignificant, even if they are not conventional successes. And you shouldn't get wrapped up in catastrophic "loser" labels or I-could-never-do-*that*-because-look-at-the-monster-I-am-now thinking because it's just not true. Trust me when I say that one day, when you are a grown-ass, overscheduled woman with a to-do list so long it makes you want to barf, you will look back on your lazy, lost "loser" days with something resembling nostalgia. Stumbling around in the world, experiencing different, not-always-pretty layers of personhood makes you well rounded and empathetic, which will work to your advantage later on. There are clues about your professional identity, what you'll love and eventually be great at, hiding in even your most seemingly defeated and underachieving times. And to really know yourself, sometimes you need to push your limits and identify what those limits are—even if you're sorting out your bottom and how low you can go.

I worked in college, just not at school. I cowrote a column in the school paper and cohosted a radio show on the college radio station. I was an RA, initially so I could scam a single dorm for free in the best building on campus, but eventually because I loved being an RA and was good at it. Sure, I did bong hits in my room, but I also connected with the women in my charge. I kept careful watch on them—not on the minimal alcohol or boys they were smuggling in, nor on the weird pets they hoarded (at a certain point, we had a scourge of ferrets on our floor), but on whether they were actually *OK*. I checked in on them, I invited them to my room for long talks, I threw floor socials, I was stern when I had to be. I was an underachiever with a piss-poor GPA, but I was also, despite myself, a person who liked and was good at being a leader.

Somewhere in that year I was arrested for staging a one-person parade in the town's Main Street, dragging sawhorses into the middle of the road and marching around, on a dare—in retrospect, an act so achingly stupid that I am almost cringing too hard right now to type. Because the street was technically part of a state highway, I was charged with obstructing state property. When they caught me, I was cuffed and thrown in a holding cell. I did and do not possess the mettle to be involved in *official situations* with *authorities*. I had finally found the limit on how much of a fuckup I could be. I could handle being a broke, stoned loser, but I did not want to ever go to jail again. It would take months of fines, numerous court dates, and endless paperwork to clear the situation up—not to mention that this would be on my record for years—but it was my last run-in with the law.

In my third year at school, when I'd long since been fired as an RA (for failing to turn in my weekly "update" paperwork on time, or really ever), I'd dropped every class except Spanish, and my midsemester report had come back with a 0.9 GPA, my parents called and said it was enough; they could not support this "effort" anymore. They would not be filling out any more financial aid forms, nor taking out any more loans. At that moment my financial profile included a few crumpled dollar bills at the bottom of my bag and couch change. I was on a payment plan for the arrest situation. It was time to make money.

CHAPTER 3

Unhappiness Cloak

My first waitressing job was at a nondescript Mexican restaurant on the lower level of a two-story strip mall on a six-lane "pike" in a nondescript Pennsylvania suburb right near a nondescript mall. We served chips and salsa and sizzling fajitas that would splatter onto the most tender parts of your neck as you balanced them high on a tray. Our house specialty was the Monstrita—a triple-serving margarita in a fishbowl-size glass with a deceptively delicate stem and the ability to get you plowed drunk within three sips. I was twenty when I got this job. I wore a black button-down man's shirt and metallic purple bolo tie. I was wobbly and awkward and not very good. The restaurant was owned by two thirtysomething Indian men, Apu and Tushar, one short and short-tempered, one tall and stoic, both fundamentally kind.

During my first week on the floor, I had a day that was particularly bad. I was working a double shift, and during lunch I spilled hot coffee on a man who was deaf. This was because I had poor balance and did not know yet how to skillfully wield a tray but also because the man was deaf, did not know I was behind him, and leaned back into the coffee as if eager to be close to a heat source.

I hadn't known you were supposed to tip the busboys, so they all hated me. As my shift progressed, all the tables in my section became dirty and nacho-strewn. Later that night I served warm chips from the wrong warm chips dispenser, the one outside, the one we were explicitly told NOT TO USE that night, and those chips turned out to have roaches in them. I spilled drinks. I slipped and broke plates. I fucked up my orders and miscalculated my checks and at the end of the fourteen-hour shift, bolo tie askew, was called into the manager's office. I was sure I was going to be fired. Instead, after acknowledging the day's disasters, Apu signaled to the bartender, who brought in two shots of tequila. He told me he knew I was trying. He said he thought I could and would get better. He told me I made the customers laugh. Then he held up the shot glass and cheered to better nights ahead. Though we both knew I'd fucked up, his approach was so empathetic and hopeful and focused on the positives, I have practiced this Apu-management method ever since.

Waiting tables was my main source of income for the next seven years.

It was the first thing in my life that gave me confidence that I could make my own way in the world. There was a hierarchy to waitressing, and I started climbing the ladder—fancier places paid more in tips and the conditions were less grueling, so I got fancy. I made Caesar salads tableside. I lit up flambés. I practiced opening champagne with a whisper and not a pop.

I learned French wines and French foods enough that I could recommend French wines and French foods. Waiting tables taught me how to talk to rich, educated people. It taught me how to move my body with strength and at least a semblance of grace. It gave me access to a sophisticated $40-an-entrée class that I would have never met otherwise. I would need to understand these people later in my career. I would need to know how to dine in places that sold $40 entrées.

For the most part, you get what you put into waitressing—the more you hustle, the more money you make. Waiting tables became the foundational education for everything I'd do in my professional life. The constant multitasking, the precision necessary to execute a meal, learning to perfect my timing and collaborate with a team—these were lessons I'd carry with me for years, and use even today. The family feeling of a restaurant, the feeling that you are all in it together, because you have to be, because you need each other to get the work done, is an apt model for team building in office jobs. Understanding the delicate ecosystem of a restaurant—who you need to take care of and give fucks about to give the customers the best experience and get the best tips—taught me how to navigate politics in big corporate jobs. In restaurants, I learned to flip power dynamics, like those of young female server versus table full of rich white businessmen. Could I wrest the power from them, let them know—subtly—that they were misogynistic assholes, and still get a good tip? Could I make them think that the $95 bottle of wine was their idea? How far could I push before it went too far, before it turned into a complaint about my "attitude"? (I got a lot of those complaints too.)

I worked in more than a dozen restaurants over the course

of my career as a waitress. The first job that profoundly changed the direction of my life was at a big hotel chain with two dining establishments.

City Limits, the classier of the two, was all 1980s pink-and-gray banquettes and soft lighting and nowhere near a city, a space where the local politicians came to cheat on their spouses (hotel rooms upstairs!), where Larry "Bud" Melman once grabbed my ass (look him up), where La Toya Jackson conducted the world's most boring conversation and ate only filet mignon. The Green Parrot was an all-you-could-eat pasta-and-crab-legs joint where bibs were provided, the gratuity was automatic, and your job as a server was to be the cleanup crew, shoveling discarded crab shells, spaghetti marinara, and blue-cheese-dressing-doused lettuce into giant trash barrels without throwing up.

When you were a new employee at this hotel, they made you work the Sunday all-you-can-eat morning buffet; when you were really new or truly loathed, you had to work Mother's Day brunch. There is no hell in the restaurant business like Mother's Day brunch. Valentine's Day, with all its forced love and romantic posturing and tables of two, sucks. New Year's Eve, when the rest of the world is out wearing sequins and blowing horns, is a sad FOMO hell. But nothing is worse than Mother's Day, with its reluctant-to-be-together families, barely-there grandmas, and feral kids running wild around hot drinks and making a mess of buffets. Mother's Day brunch customers are not mimosa and chill people. This is obligatory dining, people who don't want to be there, who aren't used to eating out, who have an unusual amount of needs, run you ragged, and then leave terrible tips. This is the lowest, messiest, busiest, cheapest, complainiest the restaurant business gets.

And this, in the sexiest of places, is where I met my first husband.

My first husband was a cute hotshot hotel manager in a place where no one was cute and no one was a hotshot. He was the popular guy in high school who would have never dated me back then. He wore man shoes and double-breasted suits from Men's Wearhouse in various shades of brown and listened to Rush in his convertible with the top down. We hung out for two months—a distraction, an East Coast summer fling—and then, when it would've been over, when we would've each moved on to people more our own kind, I got pregnant. He said he would marry me. He was kind and normal, and he wanted to marry me. I was lost and sad and broke and felt like a freak. I said yes.

Five months later we were married in a cavernous Catholic church in front of 150 of our parents' closest friends. I wore a bride costume: white gloves, a giant satin-and-sequins dress from David's Bridal and a crinoline veil spotted with faux pearls. Under my dress, I wore a pale-blue garter and an over-size sanitary pad. I was still bleeding from the miscarriage.

We spent the first few months of marriage in a small, stark town near the hotel where we worked. We rented an all-white one-bedroom apartment covered in indoor/outdoor gray carpet and furnished with leftover hotel furniture—brass and felted teal banquet chairs, a multicolored houndstooth-print sofa, bedside tables with the lamps attached. It was the setting a lo-cation scout would choose if the goal was to show characters slowly drifting into insanity, death by starkness-plus-ugliness. It was what we could afford. I picked up a second job during the day, working at a New Age coffee shop across the street from our apartment. I made cappuccinos and defrosted "grade-A" scones. I sold copies of *The Alchemist*. I led people to spirit animal workshops and tarot card readings in the events space upstairs. For our first Christmas together, my husband bought me a vacuum cleaner. I wanted a bike. We did not know each other at all.

Later that year, in the first of a series of relocations we made to try to make things right between us—because I was sure making things right between us would make me right—we moved to the attic apartment of a two-hundred-year-old bed-and-breakfast that was originally a stagecoach stop and general store for *Deadwood*-type folks traveling from Philly into as-yet-uncivilized lands. We were hired as innkeepers, though my husband kept his regular job at, and a long commute to, the hotel where we'd met. We welcomed guests traveling through rural Pennsylvania, mostly in the summer, mostly old people in shorts. We gave them breakfast and, later, led them to the tavern downstairs where they could drink Grasshoppers and dine on dishes like prime rib or crab cakes in front of a fireplace. They said the inn was haunted. They asked if I'd seen the ghosts. I would have welcomed the company.

At night I waited tables at the restaurant downstairs. I worked with women in their forties and fifties, women who talked about their husbands and kids and goulash. It was seventeen miles to the nearest store. On our first anniversary, in the dead of winter, my husband worked late. I opened a bottle of wine and watched *Love Connection* reruns on our tiny TV, snow out the windows as far as you could see.

One afternoon late that summer, while I was dusting a sitting room, the inn's main phone rang. It was my mother, calling to say she was excited about my upcoming move to Connecticut. I did not know I was moving to Connecticut. My husband had called her first to discuss his promotion—a relocation! Didn't she think that was great? She did. I did not know what I felt anymore.

Three weeks later we moved to a hotel for business travelers in Stamford, Connecticut. My husband had been sent to fix its food and beverage department. We were put up in the hotel for a period of four months, though we'd stay six. As part of his employment package or maybe just to be nice, I was hired at the hotel's revolving rooftop restaurant, Windows on the Sound, which was really Windows onto Interstate 95 with a sliver of water in the distance. Late at night, when I finished working, I would retire to our standard-size hotel room, order personal pan pizzas from the Express Pizza Hut downstairs, and eat them atop a floral-print bedspread on the king-size bed. There was no cable. We worked strange hours and were often up late. We watched a lot of *Three's Company* and a lot of info-mercials. My husband made three easy payments of $29.99 for a vibrating brush and a year's supply of hair-growth shampoo in big cardboard boxes that took up most of our bathroom. He hung the instructional poster on the wall. The shampoo smelled like old perm, and so did our room. My husband's job was more difficult than we'd imagined, or maybe he wasn't as good at it as we'd thought. Either way, he worked seventy-hour weeks. I was often, almost always, alone.

There was TV and room service. There were conventions, weekends when the hotel was flooded with pharmacists, recovery groups, accountants, dentists. There was the hotel gym, but I never went. I waited on business travelers, lonely and awkward, newspapers under their arms, before there were cell phones to keep humans company. During the day I nannied for the hotel general manager's girlfriend's kids, who had just moved to the hotel too. They lived in a suite on the twenty-second floor. The kids missed California, they missed their friends, they missed their dad. We were all strangers and nomads. The hotel restaurant revolved. Everything felt unmoored, like one day we could all float away.

When you work in the hospitality business, you are a voyeur, witnessing and even participating in some of the most intimate moments of people's lives. I watched groups of female friends celebrate birthdays together, hugging and gossiping and conspiring, getting topply and tipsy by the end of the meal. I watched anniversary weekends, men carrying women they'd loved for years over standard-hotel-room thresholds. I observed terrible and wonderful first dates, all tense until the wine started flowing, until someone made a good joke and someone else laughed. I served big family graduation and retirement dinners, wedding and baby showers, generations in attendance. I helped orchestrate elaborate engagements—*can you put the ring on the cake, can you put it in her glass of champagne, can you serve it, and just it, for dessert.* I sang "Happy Birthday" to beautiful women whose husbands signaled me nervously, tried to give the heads-up without their wives seeing, even though they nearly always did. These celebrations, these moments of joy, affection, connection, only made my loneliness more profound. I was tethered to a man I increasingly understood I did not love, living in strange places I did not like, around people I did not know. I was witness to other people's lives, but I was not living my own, and that clarified the fact that I wanted one, more desperately than I even understood.

We ran up the bill in the hotel room—too much room service, too many movies, too many long-distance calls, and, as I'd find out later, too much porn. We overstayed our welcome. We were supposed to find an apartment, but we never did. My husband got another job and we moved back to Pennsylvania, to another rural hotel, this one next to the QVC studio, where Joan Rivers would come and stay with her tiny dog and sell jewelry on TV. My husband sometimes walked her dog. He said she was nicer than she was on TV. He said Victoria Principal was a bitch, though. These are the things you remember.

Soon after, I'd be sitting in the driveway, trying to leave. Soon after that, I pulled myself together—pretty much for good.

CHAPTER 4

Let Your Dreams Slap You in the Face

There's a phenomenon that happens in the beginning of biopics, a moment when, as a child, the soon-to-be famous protagonist hits a ball out of the local ballpark, sings a note she should not be able to sing, launches an elaborately built rocket using too-sophisticated-for-her-age quantum physics, or writes her first novel, the words pouring out, perfect and pristine. It's a corny plot device, a tidy way to move along otherwise boring origin stories, a move to validate legend that this person's life was fated from the start. It was meant to be. There could be no other way.

You see this in real life too, in live interviews and in magazine profiles: successful person X explaining that she "always knew" she would do successful thing Y, that it was what she loved forever, that it shone in her face one day like a magic destiny sunbeam. "I was four, and I picked up my first tennis racket/violin/paintbrush/microphone/surfboard/chess piece; I put on the fencing mask, I jumped up on that balance beam, I got into the driver's seat of the race car. I had the feeling that I was home."

When success happens like this, it's beautiful and life-affirming, which is why we enjoy these stories as much as we do. The idea of a predetermined path gives us a sense of safety and security in a world that often feels random and senseless, a world in which us weirdos often feel lost. I believe these people when they say they always knew what they wanted to be, that they laser-focused and it all fell into place like a slo-mo video of pearly dominoes dropping in a line. But much as "meant to be" love stories about "the one" fill us with unrealistic expectations about what marriage and finding a partner are supposed to look like, finding your career path doesn't always happen this way, and imagining that it will or should can leave you feeling anxious or paralyzed, wanting to crawl into a ball and hide under the bed. It can make you feel like you shouldn't even try.

But I want you to try. I want you to get out from under the bed of fear and start living, so let's cut to the chase: it's highly unlikely that a career-path lightning bolt will hit you one day and give you road-to-success superpowers. Sometimes your career identity unfolds over years, the path twisting and turning as you learn more about both yourself and the working world. Sometimes, after decades doing something else, your brain cracks open, and you know you do not want to be a dental assistant anymore and instead need to become the world's greatest cartoonist. And sometimes finding what you should do with your life starts simply with having the courage to try something else.

None of this will be easy. All of it will require sacrifices that may at first feel unintuitive and even crazy. Especially if where you want to land is far from where you currently are. Especially if you are about to enter the business of reinvention.

Recently I sat on a porch by the Jersey shore with my mom. It was early summer, everything around us green and blooming, muggy and fertile in that way only certain parts of the world stick, and smell, in June. It was early morning. My mother was wearing a floral-print nightgown and drinking coffee out of a floral-print cup. My mother and I don't talk much about how my life unfolded. She loves me and she's proud of me, but there is a sense of loss too—I don't live near her physically or emotionally; I haven't for years. Our relationship is less consistent than either of us would like, sometimes more fragile. On this morning, my mother is rocking in a green wicker chair. We are talking about this book. She is happy I am writing it, she is overjoyed. It's what I was meant to do, she says. She always knew.

"Did you?" I say. "Did you really?" I am pushing against the falseness of this narrative, the revisionist history, the movie plot device. I want my story to be more than destiny or fate, the turn of a tarot card. I want more control and more credit. *Does she not remember how I failed?*

"Well, you won awards for writing all the time."

"I did not. I won an award once from the Daughters of the Revolution for that essay about the Revolutionary War. I was also really good at roller-skating that year, and eating pizza."

I go for the joke, but she doesn't laugh. When I was a kid, she was harder, with more edges—dark hair, dark eyes, dark olive skin, cheekbones and legs and anger and attitude for days. She's softer now, grays covered over with blond, age bringing calm. She rocks and pauses to drink her coffee, rocks and pauses.

"Well, you were always a little *different*. I always knew you were different from the other kids, different from my other kids." She doesn't remember that I was failing school and failing gym. She doesn't remember all my shitty jobs; she sees the entire period now as a life on pause, a disruption in service of my fate and path. "I don't know if you were meant to be a writer, but you were always different, I knew that for sure."

"But I didn't want to be, Mom."

After I say this, I cry harder and louder and uglier than I can remember crying in a long time.

Here's why: Even if there were no overt expectations for my life—no long line of doctors, no family business that had something to do with money, no farm—there was an unspoken assumption that as an Italian American daughter from a working-class family in a provincial Northeast American city, I'd stick close to home and to what I knew. That's what my cousins did—that's what my parents' friends' kids and almost everyone else I grew up with did. I was "different," but I hated being so, I confined myself and made "expected" choices, for a very long time. And I failed at all of them. And here is where destiny and, more important, our innermost dreams get tricky for us misfits: we often fight against them. We don't want to be weird. Leaving behind your tribe, going against convention and cultural or familial expectations, can be fundamentally, achingly lonely. It's scary at first to even imagine it.

When we talk reinvention or finding ourselves, when we hold up our modern-day Horatio Alger success stories, they're often dazzlingly positive, a sleek spread in a women's magazine, a Mary Tyler Moore–leaping story of triumph, displayed in Inspiring-with-a-capital-I Pinterest-quote light. You're following your heart! You're following your dreams! But to gain a new identity, you have to leave an old one behind. You shed skin, and you shed comfort. You shed what you know. You may become fragmented and outside yourself for a long time. Professional identity, in the beginning, can feel like a too-big suit you're trying on, an other self that you are trying to portray, like you've *Being John Malkovich*'d into a PROFESSIONAL PERSON when inside you feel like a vulnerable kid. Which means that for many of us, discovering our dreams, or even the next step to achieving success, feels less like an obvious, meant-to-be golden road laid out before us and more like an excavation of fear.

Follow Your Bad Feelings

Ultimately, the process for finding the vocation I wanted and would excel at wasn't soft or calm. It wasn't worksheets or matching my personality type against a series of careers to see what lined up. Those things never turned up "writer" or "editor"; instead they made me seem like a sociopath. And finding my "calling" wasn't even about being pragmatic and making lists of what I was good at and what interested me, what sounded compelling or fun. How I found the color of my particular parachute was by force, by taking a hard and honest look at my sadness and insecurity, what made me the most pissed off and envious, the things that I wanted to be so badly that I seethed.

And here, I am going to advise you—on top of all the

inspiring, life-affirming exercises you've found in other career books or in online quizzes or the advice you've gleaned from your dad—to follow your bad feelings and let them lead you to the BIG DREAM of what it is you want to do now. Because behind your anger and jealousy is passion, and even further behind it is fear, and these very strong feelings are what you're going to need to be persistent and unrelenting and succeed at and love what you do.

Is there a person in your life who makes you secretly feel TREMENDOUSLY jealous? Whose social media you stalk and think UGH, WHY DOES SHE GET TO DO THIS THING / I WOULD LIKE TO EAT THIS PERSON'S BRAIN AND THEN PUT ON HER CLOTHES AND COMMUTE TO HER OFFICE ON MONDAY?

Is there a job that makes you ANGRY? Fuck that stupid website. Fuck that architecture firm. Fuck that lady helping people at that place. Fuck those people who work for that designer. Fuck her for getting to write a book. Fuck Snapchat, it looks like a ridiculous place to work. Fuck fuckin' fuck.

Now listen with more intention, because probably what you're actually hearing is: *I wish that were me.* And instead of wasting all this time being jealous, sad, or pissed, you should channel that energy into transforming your life.

When I was in college the first time, I had a friend, writing partner, and, later, nemesis named Sylvia. Sylvia and I had the kind of tumultuous, dysfunctional, codependent girl friendship that's almost tragic-romantic, that sparks petty jealousies, ferocious competition, devastating rejection, and near-constant high-drama arguments. The kind of friendship that always

comes back to do it all over again, until one day it doesn't anymore. Until one day it breaks your heart.

Whereas I had spent a childhood trying to pass as normal,
Sylvia was FULL WEIRDO, and proud of it. She wore messy,
thick winged eyeliner and giant flatform boots and home-
made chandelier earrings and long hippie skirts that dragged
on the ground behind her when she walked. She read poetry
and smoked cigarettes and was always sewing something into
her long, pretty hair. She was brilliant and deep and thrilling,
fearless and unexpected, and she always said what was on her
mind. Sometimes I couldn't believe I got to know her, to be
close to her. She was creative beyond measure and totally, specially messed up. I loved her more than I have loved almost
anyone else in my life.

We wrote a weekly, co-bylined column for the school paper
together in the same room, at the same table, sometimes dic-
tating each sentence to the other into an old word processor. As
a writer and editor, Sylvia was sure-footed; I was insecure and
panicked. We fought and fought and fought during the process.
I thought she was better than me, more natural and original.
These feelings made me feel *bad*. These feelings made me jealous and angry. They made me want to totally give up. And for a
long time, I did. I did not know yet that there was room for all
different types of writers; I did not understand that I could get
better. Back then, I understood the world as either/or, black/
white, good/shit. But if I had listened to those feelings and ex-
amined what was underlying how horrible they made me feel,
it might not have taken me a decade to pursue what I wanted to
do. And I might not have let my insecurity, my jealousy—over

writing, boys, Sylvia's presence on the planet as a unique and confident human—ruin our friendship in the process.

So here is my advice for finding what you want to do: Roll around in the world, examine what you like and what you don't, study what comes naturally to you and what doesn't. Follow your bad feelings to their origin. Lift up the rock of your envy of that girl who makes textiles/writes graphic novels/builds buildings/takes pictures. Expose yourself. Get to a place where you are vulnerable and open. In this journey of exploration, there may come a moment when what you want to do will slap you in the face, when doing this thing and imagining yourself doing this thing will feel so special as to almost be illicit, and when thinking about getting paid just for doing this thing will nearly kill you with happiness. When someone else is doing what you want to do, you will blaze with jealousy. It will burn and burn and burn inside you. Actually doing what you want to do will make you feel so afraid your body will shake, and you will want to throw up. Whether your career dream is specific or broad, creative or medical or political or technical, gaining access to this dream will feel exhilarating. This is how you know you've found it.

Now you've got to ask yourself some hard questions.

Some Hard Questions

What Kind of Training Do You Need to Do This Thing?

So now you know what you want to do. Start looking at job listings for the jobs you want, at the entry level: What are the requirements? Do you fit those requirements? Can you bend your own training/experience to meet at least the minimum? If not, you should sort out precisely the training you'll need—the MBA, the MFA, the teacher's certification, the specialist's license. You should identify places where you can get this training and start applying now. Don't say you're too old, don't say it will take three years and by the time you're done you'll be twenty-six, or thirty-four, or forty-one. Barring some seriously bad shit, you'll turn twenty-six or thirty-four or forty-one anyway. You'll feel a lot better about yourself if you accomplish something in those years, rather than staying stuck where you are right now.

Don't tell yourself that school is too expensive. You can find a way. There are loans, and there is aid. Trust me when I say you will be happier in a fulfilling career, having accomplished your goals, with a $300-a-month student loan payment, than you will having done nothing at all, having never tried, having given over your life to mediocre work that makes you feel dead inside.

Where Do You Want to Live?

Not all, but many professions are concentrated in certain areas of the country. Sure, you *can* be a software engineer for a digital company in North Carolina, but you are going to have scads more options and opportunities if you live in Northern California. Do you like fashion? It's mainly in New York. Film and television are mainly in LA. While newspapers and magazines and websites are all over, there's nothing as exhilarating as working in media in New York. If you want to totally immerse yourself in a professional experience, if you want a multitude of companies and positions around you and lots of peers to bounce ideas off, brainstorm with, and make you better at what you do, it's a good idea to move to the place where there are the most of you doing that thing.

How Do You Feel about Money?

Money will not buy anywhere close to happiness, obviously. And it should not be the primary factor when you are sorting out what you want to do. In fact, there's a thing I read once that says once you make $70,000 a year—or once your basic needs are met, with a cushion of security—more money does not equal any more life satisfaction. However, if you are a person who likes stuff, expensive stuff—nice cars, fancy vacations, designer bags—you might want to rethink your career as a preschool teacher (honorable, amazing, beautiful work that should pay more than it does). It's important to be realistic with yourself about money, how important it is to you, and what your earning potential could be in different careers.

For example, I don't need a lot of money—I'm not a person who ever cared about or wanted to be rich—but I like to be able to go out and blow money on cash-fire nonessentials like overpriced beverages and keep up my addiction to buying $37 vintage dresses on eBay. Unlike many of my peers, when I was starting out, I was never going to be parentally subsidized; the freelance hustle always terrified me, and I found sanity-making comfort in regular paychecks and full benefits. Which meant that I had to earn more to be comfortable, which meant that when I was sorting out my career, I knew I could not be a straight visual artist or a poet (classes I took, careers I considered). Which means I've taken jobs in my profession that didn't totally excite me because they've paid well. Which means that, in order to earn more money, I've been a bit of a sellout.

If you want to earn a certain amount of money—if you have financial considerations like significant student loan debt, or you're a parent, or you're taking care of sick parents—you will have to factor this into decisions about your dream career and the pace of pursuing it. Because no matter how much you love what you do, if you're terrified about your ability to pay your bills and there's very little shot of you making more, over time, your life is going to become very stressful and unpleasant. I am not saying that money should be your main motivator. Some people, people I know and love well, are not motivated by money at all. They have three shirts and enough to pay rent and a bit of a freegan spirit and are perfectly content. But understanding your relationship with money and your lifestyle expectations should be a factor you consider as you move into a career.

What Kind of Life Do You Want?

Do you want to work from home, or in an office? Or a combination of these two?

How much are you willing to work? There are "always on" careers that require all of your time and some of your soul— digital publishing, start-ups, political campaigns, law offices with big cases, jobs in medicine (I assume, from what I've seen on *Grey's Anatomy*), TV writing and producing (at least for a few months a year). If you are not suited to being on call and never truly turning off work, you will resent the hell out of these jobs. Can you work in a formal office environment with a strict dress code and rigid rules about decorum? Or are you a rules-breaking person who'd be better suited to owning your own winter sport supply shop and teaching kids to snowboard? This is the moment to be as honest with yourself as you can.

After my failed attempt to leave my husband, I started asking myself these questions. I thought hard and long about what I actually wanted. By then we were living in a college town (for those keeping score, we lived in six places in four different states in the three years we were married). I was taking English lit classes, and I'd started writing the tiniest bit for the local paper, which didn't pay and didn't edit, so if you turned in a story with a typo, it was printed that way. But I liked it. And I obsessed over it. And I read the words I'd written over and over, and each time it gave me a thrill. The thrill I felt from writing felt secret and vital. It lit me up like nothing else up until that point had. This was a clue, and I followed it.

I also knew I wanted to get the hell out of Pennsylvania and start fresh in a new city. New York seemed impossible—too big, too intimidating. I needed a baby step. I'd been to Boston once. It looked like Philly, but smaller and cleaner. The people seemed fancier. I liked the ducks. I applied to Emerson College's Writing, Literature and Publishing program that spring. My thinking was that if writing didn't work out for me, I could learn enough to go into the business of publishing things, which would keep me around writers and writing. This would be close enough. Miraculously, given my for-shit GPA, I was accepted (I wrote a pleading essay about how I wanted to turn my life around; it worked). My husband was on board for the adventure—we moved to Boston that summer.

Boston was the one last geographic in my disintegrating marriage, the last shot to make everyone happy and make things work. We moved to a tiny studio apartment in Boston's North End, on the Freedom Trail (a metaphor that does not escape me now), right across the street from Paul Revere's house. I got a job serving sangria to college-age Europeans. Emerson's campus was sprinkled all over the city, in various beautiful brownstone buildings, a real leafy college experience to call my own. I felt *lucky* to be there. I was so grateful to be learning. I felt like I was stealing something. I rode my bike in the crisp autumn all over the city, crossing the Charles River and back, riding through stately Back Bay. I was happy; my husband was not. We broke up six months later. When we divided our marital assets, he let me take a set of silverware and a futon. I tried to smuggle out a drinking glass. It slipped out of my bag as I was leaving, and my husband picked it up and brought it inside, closing the door behind him as he went.

I worked or went to school constantly. I moved into an apartment three blocks away, above an Italian bakery, with two eccentric women and a Siamese cat. It would take years for the divorce to be finalized—getting divorced is a hundred times more complicated than getting married—but I was free.

During this time, if a customer or a professor or a fellow student used a word I didn't understand—which was often—I wrote it down. Later, after getting home from my restaurant shift, I looked it and others up in a dictionary. I made sample sentences, and said those sentences aloud long into the night. I quizzed myself the next day. I scribbled down every book or magazine or NPR show or movie mentioned in any conversation with smart people, and looked them up and read or watched or listened to them too. I got straight As. I went to school for twenty-six continuous months, taking full course loads year-round while holding down a full-time waitressing schedule.

And then, at the end of it all, I tried to find a "real" job.

PART II

Embrace Your
Weird

CHAPTER 5

Don't Fake It Till
You Make It

like to trot out the fact that I went on twenty-three interviews before I landed my first job in New York media. It's a number I remember all these years later because, in the late 1990s and early '00s, because I was insecure, shit-scared, and looking for tidy patterns in a life that felt both directionless and navel-gaze fascinating, I kept copious notes on every aspect of my life—bus rides I took, customers I waited on, humans I made out with, T-shirts I liked a lot. More than the rest, I'm glad I remember the interview number. It's a crowd-pleaser; it makes me seem like the kind of plucky go-getter whose stick-to-itiveness and staying power will propel her to success, even when the chips are down. This representation is both true and not true. Once I figured out what I wanted to do, I was determined to Make It Happen. Each awkward, not-connecting interview and coinciding rejection was a blow to my ego that made me more and more resolute. I was tired of failing, and I was not going to let all these people keep me from my dreams.

But this does not mean I deserved to get those first twenty-three jobs that I did not get. When I talk about my "journey" to "success," a sizable percentage of what I attribute to tenacity was, in reality, the confidence of ignorance. I was confident that I could pull a fast one on the hiring people by transforming myself into what I thought they wanted. I was ignorant of my inherent value, of what made me a uniquely appealing and actually hirable candidate—and as a result, I prolonged the job search process by weeks, if not months.

I'm not saying there's anything wrong with determination and just hard-core wanting it more than anyone else, but the reason I didn't get nearly two dozen jobs after nearly two dozen grueling interviews was in large part because I was misrepresenting myself. I was faking it to make it, but the faking did not make anything happen. This might be because I'm a bad faker, but it's more likely that this faking-it business is a bad idea. My phoniness read in my résumé, and it showed in my interviews. My story of twenty-three interviews is a fun one to dine out on, but it was not a fun one to live.

Here Is the Actual Truth about Résumés and Cover Letters*

Now that you know what you want to do, it's time to outmuscle all your worthlessness fears, to hold your nose and close your

---

* I'm adding a few obligatory sentences about cover letters in the gutter here because we should not waste real page space on them. Like résumés, cover letters are mostly procedural bullshit. People rarely write good ones because the entire setup is far too stiff and contrived. Your cover letter should be short and to the point. You should state your relevant experience, say something that shows you understand

eyes, or whatever it is you need to do to momentarily defeat the insecurity monster and go after that first gig.*

But before that, you'll have to create your résumé.†

There are tons of sites, books, coaches, and even classes that will teach you the ins and outs of how to make a résumé and help you productively procrastinate, fall down a rabbit hole, and overthink the entire enterprise. But here are the only two things you really need to know.

1. Résumés are mostly bullshit, and no one reads them.
2. In that résumés are not bullshit, the only things hiring/setting-up-interview people are looking for, in order of importance, are:

    a. where you've worked;
    b. how long you worked there;
    c. your title(s);
    d. where you went to school and what degree(s) you earned; and
    e. what year you graduated, so they can figure out your age (they can't legally ask, and they might want to know for a number of reasons, including to decide if

---

the company/position, be enthusiastic and gracious. Don't overstate what you do, write more than three short paragraphs, be overly kiss-assy or effusive. Read your cover letter aloud—does it sound annoying? Rewrite it until it does not. Now cut it down again. Send it. Try not to obsess or feel bad about yourself. The end. Now back to the truly fascinating topic of résumés.

*   Youngs: All of this advice applies to internships too.

†   Some people call résumés CVs, but the two are not interchangeable—CVs are longer, more detailed documents that are focused on academic experience and mainly used in Europe. Do not make a CV unless someone asks you to, you are a European person, or you want to come off as very formal and maybe a wee bit pretentious.

your age makes them like you more or less; because,
yes, this process is obviously less cool than you'd like).

That's it. I say this with all compassion and love, not only
because I care whether you get a job, but also because I want
to save the world from bad résumés. The people fielding hundreds of these documents are not looking at all the fluffed-up
responsibilities you've put in there, or all those formal, only-
used-on-résumés verbs like *liaised*. And no matter how pretty
and how flowery you've made "organizing stuff" and "setting
up meetings" sound, the person reading your résumé has also
organized things and shepherded humans into rooms, and it
is so much better, in this, your seconds-long first impression,
to be clear and direct and honest and not try to turn "makin'
doughnuts" into "doughnut artist," which is a thing that I actually saw on a résumé from a person applying for a job that had
nothing to do with doughnuts or food.

Don't freak out about your résumé. Don't agonize and then
avoid it for three weeks because it is too much and—gah—you
feel paralyzed and maybe you should just live with your parents forever. It's not too much. It's annoying, but it's simple.
Yours should be neatly laid out in chronological order on *one
page* (you don't need two pages unless maybe you are Hillary
Clinton—and even then . . .). It shouldn't include an objective;
for the love of God, your objective is obviously to find a job.
There should be no tricks or lies or exaggerations on it; not only
do you have a moral obligation to be honest, but in the trans-
parent interwebs times we live in now, fibs and stretches are
way more trouble than they're worth. And it should be printed
in a font that does not call to mind a flyer for a children's birth-

day party in 1987. Your résumé doesn't need to showcase your unique personality or spot-on aesthetic, unless the job you are applying for is all about the way things look. It should read just smart and relevant enough that someone will click on it and say, "My, look at this fine young person. Let's bring her in and find out more about her!" (Or, in reality: "This person doesn't look insane—let's bring her in.")

The fact that I got twenty-three interviews off my bizarrely formatted, jazz-handing résumé of lies is a testament to both dumb luck and the goodwill bubble that surrounds you sometimes when your intentions are pure and your will is strong. It is a testament to the good work of the Radcliffe—now Columbia—Publishing Course that I enrolled in with the last of my waitressing money right before moving to New York, a course that spends six weeks teaching rubes like me about the publishing business, particularly how to network. Most profoundly, my getting interviews was a testament to my privilege as a white person. Even if I felt like I did not fit in classwise, even if in every networking event I felt more comfortable talking to the waitstaff than the community of professionals I was trying to engage, I was a white girl with a white-sounding name entering into a profession of mostly white people. I didn't have a pedigree, I didn't have connections, I had not attended a school starting with an H or a Y. I was awkward, rough around the edges, unrefined; but still—and this cannot be underestimated—I was straight, white, cis, and able-bodied in a world stacked in favor of straight, white, cis, able-bodied people, and on those terms alone, I passed. Things were not easy for me, but my bootstrap story would have been infinitely harder without this privilege, in ways I can't pretend to understand.

The world is changing—it's changed in the years since I started working—but it's not changing fast enough. People will be shitty and make assumptions about you because of where you come from and what you look like. They will make you feel small and bad. But know this: You can fulfill your dreams with or without their approval. You can surpass those people, and you will. There was a mildly sociopathic exercise I employed in the early years of my career, every time someone made me feel small. Every time someone, usually a rich white man, corrected my malapropisms in a condescending way; every time someone, usually a rich white woman, told me it would be "great" if I dressed better when I barely had enough money to eat; every time someone demeaned or degraded me under the guise of "constructive criticism," but really because something about me made them uncomfortable, made them need to have power over me, I stared and nodded, acknowledging them silently, while repeating over and over in my head: *I'll surpass you.*

Over time, I did.

What Not to Do: My Dumb First Résumé

Here is an annotated version of my résumé in the summer/fall of 2000.

Intern, the *Beacon Hill Paper*

Though touted on my résumé as a "local newspaper," in truth the *Beacon Hill Paper* was more of a newsletter made in the basement/former servants' quarters of a multistory house in the leafy, bricky Boston neighborhood of Beacon Hill, which seemed to have been leafy, bricky, and full of quietly rich white people since the beginning of time. Run by an energetic middle-aged white lady named Lotti, who'd lived in the same house her entire life, the *Beacon Hill Paper* mostly covered society happenings in Beacon Hill, community issues around things like fire hydrants and jaywalking, the occasional obituary, and anything about the arts that could have been written in either 1998 or 1908. Once the paper featured a multiweek series about a naughty neighborhood cat. Though my résumé exaggerated my experience there, including reporting chops ("broke stories on neighborhood happenings") and editing ("weekly features on prominent community members and issues critical to the community"), I mainly reported, wrote, and edited lots of event listings for the calendar page.* Like many *New Yorker*–hoarding ladies living in large houses with original colonial furniture in small American cities in the late 1990s, Lotti had significant social aspirations and was concerned about getting the "right" people in the paper and highlighting the "right" events—she went to great lengths to make our paper the paper of record in Beacon Hill. I was more interested in the freaky underground of the neighborhood, namely the four or five 1960s bohemians who'd managed to stow away in rent-controlled apartments as the area became unspeakably rich.

One of these bohemians was John Wieners, an obscure Beat poet who hung with Allen Ginsberg and Lawrence Ferlinghetti

---

* I do not wish events-listings writing and editing on anyone on earth, though if there is a better exercise to simultaneously teach on-the-phone reporting ("Hello? WTF is this event, sir?"), mundane fact-checking ("And it's Tuesday at 7:00 p.m. at which exact address?"), writing with brevity (print = limited space), and the fact that you will have to eat a bunch of shit before you get to do what you want (listings are tedious and never-ending), I don't know it.

back in the day, worked at City Lights Bookstore in San Francisco in the 1950s, and, after suffering several nervous breakdowns, now resided in a tiny, cluttered apartment on Joy Street in Beacon Hill. I stalked Wieners for six months before finally getting him to agree to an interview for the *BHP*. I waited outside his apartment, I called his home phone; I even creeped on and struck up relationships with his remaining local friends, who were odd and a little sad but mostly wonderful and warm old poets, one of whom served me tuna casserole in his rundown studio apartment and regaled me with dirty stories about Jack Kerouac, which may or may not have been true. Eventually, after all this prodding, Wieners agreed to the interview. When he showed up to the chosen meeting spot (his choice—an old-timey diner by the Charles River that smelled like burned coffee and was decorated as if a Creamsicle had blown up inside), he was more frail than I'd imagined, disheveled, and wearing all of his clothes inside out. Instead of greeting me, he dumped the graying tote bag he was carrying onto the table, tumbling out what looked like a decade's worth of assorted yellowed mail. He proceeded to sort through this pile, mute, while I plied him with questions straight out of Journo 101, most of which he ignored. I was unprepared for him, unprepared for anything raw or human or unexpected. I needed this to look like it did on TV. I had not done the right research. Wieners's bag also contained an array of tattered personal photos—had I known more, I would have tuned in, asked better questions about them; had I known more, I would have let the scene unfold around me, done more research, interviewed his friends, and tried to create a portrait of a smart, complicated, and obviously troubled human and pitched it somewhere it could be published with dignity. Instead, we ran the piece as a three-inch-long profile of a "colorful neighborhood character," most likely next to another story about that darn cat. Wieners died four years later; I was among the last "journalists" to speak with him. It was a missed opportunity, and one of the first lessons I had about being out of my depth and not always being able to fake it.

Intern, the *Boston Phoenix*/Stuff @Night

There was a time, not so long ago, before that Robert De Niro/ Anne Hathaway movie and before interns were actually paid, when an internship could mean basically anything. You'd find an available position from a drawer in the college career center, and you'd use an old-timey phone to call the place up, and then possibly be assigned a department and have someone in that department sign a form. When you showed up, sometimes no one knew you were coming and you'd have literally zero work to do and you'd have to fend for yourself among a group of busy professional people who were annoyed that you were there, that you were young, that their jobs sucked. I am sure I was *technically* hired as an intern at the *Boston Phoenix* in 1997; if not, I wouldn't have been let into the office and wouldn't know that in 1997, you could still smoke inside. But I showed up two or three times, tops, for two or three hours at a time, and the only mark I left on the place were a few cigarettes in the smoking-lounge ashtray.

Freelance writer, *Boston Magazine*

I was hardly a regular "freelance writer." I had two published stories in *Boston Magazine*. One, a 250-word gossip item on Arnold Schwarzenegger and Hard Rock Cafe, was a bylined, in-print piece that was entirely rewritten by a member of the magazine's staff. The second was a feature in the special Boston "Homes" edition about elaborate aquariums rich people were getting built into their houses, which I was assigned because literally no one else would take it, and for which I interviewed approximately two hundred people and visited seventeen homes and aquariums within the Boston and surrounding areas. (When it came time to write the thing, I had no idea which details were important and which were not, having made a rookie writer mistake that you should not make: don't report too little, but don't report too much either, because you will lose all focus on the thing, and transcribing and writing will make you wish for your own death.) Beyond that, my time at *Boston Magazine* involved hanging out with one of its young staff writers, cleaning out his desk, and helping him "report" on things like test-driving luxury vehicles.

This "freelance writer" exaggeration came back to bite me months later, in an interview with an editor who wanted to hire me for a junior-level job that would require a lot of writing. Though I'd sent the editor my aquarium and Arnold clips, since I'd been a "freelance writer" who wrote "regularly," he wanted to see more writing samples. I had to tell him that was the whole kitty. An awkward conversation ensued. I did not get the job.

Office Manager, Michael Mayer Photo Studio

Fearing that I lacked administrative experience (which I did—when I finally landed a job, I didn't even know how to work the printer), I also included on my résumé this gem, which unless the "Studio" was our sparsely furnished two-room Boston apartment, and unless you'd count getting stoned and watching *Party of Five* reruns from our futon bed "managing an office," this was no job at all. Though we'd broken up years before, I called my ex-boyfriend Michael Mayer, instructed him that he might be needed as a reference, and reminded him about all those months that I paid the rent with my waitressing money when he was broke and also that he'd been a shitty boyfriend who cheated on me with a Swedish model. Fabricating a job was among the more idiotic things I've done. It's a miracle I didn't get caught. And, as it turned out, none of it was necessary—and none of it was worth it.

Weird in a World of Interviews

I was still living in Boston at the time I started interviewing—about four and a half hours from New York City (where most of the jobs were, and where I wanted to be) by bus or train or car, though the train was out of the question financially, and I hadn't had a car since my '88 Nissan Sentra from my first go-round at college. So I'd try to pack in as many interviews as I could in one or two days, and I'd take the Peter Pan bus down from Boston once a week, wearing my suit pants and a tank top and flip-flops. In my bag—a red-and-black hiking backpack—I carried the suit's matching blazer, a vintage ladies' briefcase, and too-high heels from Designer Shoe Warehouse that made my feet bleed upon contact but were what I thought fancy ladies at magazines wore.

As for the suit, I'd gotten it on sale for 75 percent off at Ross Dress for Less. It was a black polyester three-button style with straight-leg slacks. It was the warmest, itchiest, and perhaps most uncomfortable thing I'd squeezed my young body into up until that point, and this was coming from a person who waited tables in hot pants and a sequined vest. But I thought black slacks suits were just how it was done—there was no one to tell me otherwise—and so it went, interview after sweaty interview.

A few weeks after I started interviewing, in the dead middle of August in New York City, five of my friends who were also interviewing for publishing jobs—some of whom were applying for the exact same jobs—and I rented a room in the Chelsea Hotel so we could stay in the city longer and go on interview "sprints." Our room was on the fifth floor of the hotel. It had fading lime-green walls and two double beds, the world's tiniest kitchen, and a cot. We were five or six in all, a mix of girls and gay men, and we all smoked cigarettes and drank until we couldn't see and shared one shower and one iron and watched from a fat, wide TV mounted high on the wall as Al Gore became the Democratic nominee at the Democratic National Convention. I loved New York that week—I loved its sweaty summery rankness, its tunnels, its dark bars, its secret corners. I knew New York was the right place for me; I just had to find a way for it to let me in.

During those summer weeks, I interviewed at *Teen People*, *Glamour*, *Interview*, and *Paper* magazines, *TV Guide*, *Esquire*, *Men's Journal*, the *New York Press*, *Sports Illustrated*, Penguin, Random House, Simon & Schuster, *Business Week*, Sexy Lad Mag 1 that no one remembers, Sexy Lad Mag 2 that no one remembers, a publishing house that I don't remember, and several more magazines that no longer exist. I interviewed with intense book editor Judith Regan; I interviewed to be Scott Rudin's assistant, a job that was, at the time, notoriously among the worst in New York. I walked into tiny offices and giant ones, I made my way through awkward security checks, I saw light-less office nooks where, if I got the job, I would be made to sit and where the current people sitting looked broken and wan, as if they'd been parked there a decade ago and never released.

In my interviews, I'd be offered water, and in attempting to drink water, I'd momentarily forget where my mouth was or what it should do; I'd dribble, my hands would shake. I rendered drink straws into miniature Carcosas, and Styrofoam cups into elaborate fingernail-imprinted sculptures (which is why I never accept beverages in interviews to this day). I sat in design-y HR waiting rooms, waiting for intimidatingly tall HR women with oversize round black glasses and graphic houndstooth-check blazers to look me up and down and explain that they'd call me, they really would, if anything came up.

When HR interviews actually led to a meeting with editors, I was told that I wasn't what they were looking for, that I didn't have enough experience, that I wasn't a "fit." Once, during an interview for an entry-level job at a magazine, I was asked if I liked books or magazines better. When I said "Magazines," the glossy-lipped twenty-five-year-old interviewer winced and said, "That's a shame, we were looking for someone who could read."

When things went well, I received follow-up interviews or editing tests—I'd get mock magazine pages and be asked to fill in what I would say about mascara X and face cream Y—what was my unique take on this lip gloss? How would I punch up the copy? I fucked these all up. I know this because the people in charge told the person who'd recommended me that I fucked it up. It was all harder than it looked, maybe I was no good at it. Maybe I should die in a fire. All of the above.

Two months into my job hunt, I ran out of money. I actually had negative money—I owed my Boston roommate for past bills and past rent, and she was (rightfully) over me, so I packed all my stuff up and moved back to Philly, in with my parents. I was a broke twenty-seven-year-old divorcee living with my parents. Are there situations more demoralizing than being a broke, in-debt twenty-seven-year-old divorcee living in your parents' attic? Of course. But I knew that was the bottom for me. I knew that if I did not get a job, there was a very real risk that soon the casual temping I'd begun in downtown Philly every day—literally pushing papers on a cart from one department to another in the basement of a cable-company's headquarters after my dad dropped me off in the morning—would become a permanent condition. There had to be more.

That was when Inside.com called.

Inside.com was a website start-up in the first bubble of start-ups, a site about the business of media and entertainment founded by veteran New York editors Kurt Andersen and Michael Hirschorn and loaded with an impossibly smart and hardworking staff of up-and-coming media stars. As the name implied, it was insidery. I did not understand what they did at all.

The office for Inside.com was located in far west Manhattan, a block away from the Hudson River, off which winds would whoosh and swirl around the tall buildings and the wide streets and, in the cold, into your bones on the long walk from the subway. In late 2000, this part of the city was still a no-man's-land, desolate both night and day, with nothing pulsing for blocks.

The office itself was a giant tech-boom 1.0 loft, with writers, editors, programmers, and designers corralled in separate playpen-like coops next to a wall of windows that revealed the western and southern edges of the city, the river, New Jersey, and beyond. It contained two conference rooms—one normal-human-size, and one circular and seven feet in diameter, literally a floor-to-ceiling blue fiberglass tube. It was the office you'd concoct in a dream in a movie about kooky Internet offices. It was the office that would change everything for me.

My cover letter for the Inside.com job was the most honest I'd written up to that point. Rather than plumping my meager résumé, I copped to having an unconventional path and highlighted my life experience and my enthusiasm for the field. I got an interview because the assistant reading the cover letters* thought I sounded cool. The fact that it was my authenticity that got me an interview is a lesson that has stuck with me ever since.

When I arrived at the office for my interview, I was led to the blue-tube conference room. A design flaw of the tube (which I'd later exploit as an assistant by scheduling intentionally uncomfortable meetings there) was that it was virtually airless. It was so hot inside that I began sweating almost immediately and had to remove my polyester blazer. I'd forgotten to shave my armpits and, not knowing how this would play at the *business website* filled with *businessmen*, kept my arms at my sides, which made me uncomfortable and annoyed. Turned out, the guy who was interviewing me—Richard, who would go on

---

* I still think cover letters are bullshit in 2017. In 2000, they were sometimes, *sometimes* relevant. This was one of those times.

to be an amazing boss and mentor—was annoyed too. Curmudgeonly by nature, he'd been looking for an assistant for longer than he deemed acceptable and was over the interviewing process. I was over it as well. After scanning my résumé, Richard's opening move was to insult my college—"So what's this school that no one's heard of?"—and push the paper over to me. "Just because you haven't heard of it doesn't mean it's not a good school," I responded, and pushed my résumé back at him. It went on like this. Looking back, I think we both recognized that the interview process was contrived, and we were both hot and annoyed, but, most important, we liked each other; we had genuine chemistry. After ten minutes, I knew I'd gotten the job.

A day later Richard called and told me I had. Four days later, I moved to New York.

In the years since, I've given a great deal of thought to that interview with Richard, the one that ended the most demoralizing job search I've endured and jump-started my life. I've come to a few conclusions that I hope will be helpful to you too. First, don't fake it until you make it. Sure, fake feeling more confident than you do, fake using a real-person voice when you want to use a robot voice, fake that you know what to do with your hands. But, in interviews especially, it's crucial that you accurately represent what it is you can and cannot do. If you once wrote a few listicles on Bernie Sanders, don't call yourself a "political reporter," just say what you did in as straightforward a way as possible. Don't oversell yourself. A smart boss will see right through it and will not hire you; a less smart boss will believe you and expect you to flex those skills on day one, and you will start your job on the wrong foot and perhaps never recover. You have merit as precisely what you are at this moment. Stick with that.

What I didn't realize during my initial job search, what would have been critical to my success and made the whole process a hundred times easier: I actually had something unique to offer at the entry level. I was underselling my real strengths with a silly, trumped-up résumé and overly formal cover letters. If, in interviews, I had actually asked about what editorial assistant jobs entailed, if I'd been less awkward, I would have seen that I had years of real-life working experience, much more than most of the entry-level candidates I was competing against. I'd been working since I was thirteen; I had been a waitress in multiple states and multiple cities, and I knew how to talk to people. I was excellent at multitasking and prioritizing, and I was good in a crisis—years in the restaurant business had taught me how to deal when something was literally on fire. I was honest, driven, extremely hardworking, grateful, didn't take any opportunity for granted. All of these qualities made me a unique, attractive candidate for the right boss. And Richard turned out to be the precise right boss. He didn't want to talk to people, he had a good sense of humor and a good eye for bullshit, he was new to his job and learning as he went, and he was kind and patient with me and my foibles. When I think about him now, and I think about that entire job, I feel so much warmth, affection, and deep gratitude. I entered that situation authentically, I worked hard, I made connections—like Richard, like the wonderful editor and writer Sara Nelson, like the late, great reporter David Carr—who would go on to be impossibly generous with me and invaluable to my career.

Though I didn't know it at the time, I would meet my future husband—the person with whom, a decade later, I'd go on to have my first kid—at Inside.com. Looking back, I cannot imagine what my life would be without that job, what my life would be if I'd given up before interview number twenty-four.

So here's another lesson: I didn't entirely understand what Inside.com was when I arrived (don't do this, obviously), and it wasn't my first, third, or even tenth choice for a first job. But it was perfect for me. It was among the best things that ever happened to my life, which goes to show that we don't always know what we need, we don't always know what's right, until it happens, and that humility and openness to different outcomes and possibilities might actually be the most important qualities you can have as you search for your first (and third, and even final) job.

Here's Where I Tell You a Bunch of Secrets about Interviews

The interview process leaves big room for missteps, misunderstanding, feelings of rejection—there's this false sense that if you could just do the perfect thing at the perfect time you could make this all better, you could get the job, you could force a desired outcome. There's a false sense of control, when actually you have very little. But landing a job is about a million more things than you and your résumé and your performance in that moment. And beyond common sense, there are no hard-and-fast rules to interviewing, no matter how many online blogs and job coaches say there are. I've seen horribly unqualified candidates land jobs there's no way in hell's deepest fire they deserve. I've watched talented candidates with perfect experience be rejected because there were four words on their résumé that the CEO of the company saw and did not like. (The four words? "Hate-watching bad TV" under "Interests." The CEO did not feel this represented the "spirit" of the company.)

Beyond actually having the right experience for a job and knowing the right person to get your foot in the door, much of interview success comes down to luck and timing—a favorite candidate with more experience dropped out because of X reason, and you were next in line; you met the boss when he/she was having a great day; the person before you was THE WORST and you are a breath of fresh air. Or, it's the opposite: the person who came in before you was Tina Fey, Amy Poehler, and Michelle Obama rolled into one, and your interview is a courtesy just in case the Amy-Tina-Mobama super candidate says no. These precise situations happen all the time, and there is nothing you can do. You can think of this situation as maddening and give up, or you can turn it on its side and get very chill about the flow of life and feel a sense of peace and liberation that very little is in your control; life is a river; this too will change; and another job, a better job opportunity, is right around the corner.

There's an embarrassing glut of articles online about interviewing; internet-y lists that say "HOW TO WIN AN INTERVIEW" in a Monster Truck voice. But I find the people who follow this kind of generic advice often feel stiff and weird IRL. They shake hands *too* firmly, they make eye contact *too* much, they're *too jazzed*. As an interviewer, I want to see *you*. I want a glimpse of who you are and how you work and what you prioritize in your professional life, what makes you feel excited and proud.

Be yourself! Lighten up! These interviews are often tedious, time-consuming, and annoying for the people doing the interviewing, most of whom are not professional HR or "talent acquisition" but normals like you and me, with another job they need to be doing. And, depending on the company, the interview process can be extra-specially daunting, with official forms to fill out, hiring panels to attend, arguments to be made for their candidate, explaining to people who actually have no idea how to do the job they're hiring for why their person is right for that job.

Case in point. Here's a secret form I got my grubby hands on that shows what happens behind the scenes in an interview at a big corporation.

CANDIDATE EVALUATION FORM

To be filled out by a minimum of five qualified manager-level or above in department.

Interviews are your chance to really dig in and examine whether each candidate has what it takes to be a top performer at _____. Think of the interview as an opportunity to promote a great workplace and evangelize the _____ brand. Interviewing is a team responsibility, and all team members are expected to stay committed to the process throughout the full cycle, until final selection occurs.

Interviewer Name: _____

Please use objective criteria when providing feedback.

Please complete within 24 hours of the interview.

Candidate Name: _____

Job Title: _____

Hiring Standards: Experience, Achievements, Potential, Collaborations and Culture Catalyst

All Ratings should be based on assessment of the candidate's Experience, Achievements, Potential, Collaboration and Culture Catalyst.

Experience
Strengths
Area of Concern

Please indicate if there are concerns about this candidate's ability to do the job, Adding an area of concern does not necessarily mean a "no" recommendation for this candidate.
Would you be an advocate for this candidate?
Are you willing to advocate for the candidate in this role?

In other words, is there an overwhelming imperative to hire this person? If yes, state the candidate's unique strengths for the role.

If this role manages people, please review The Habits of Great Managers and answer the following:

How has the candidate demonstrated great people management in their past roles, and what was key to their success? Please indicate how the candidate's people management skills will translate successfully within _____'s culture, Habits of a Great Manager, and processes/practices.

If you feel the candidate is not the right fit for this role, would you recommend they be considered for another role within the company? If yes, what organization, role, and level would you suggest?

OVERALL CANDIDATE HIRING RECOMMENDATION

OVERALL RATING

4.0 = Exceptionally qualified—MUST HIRE

3.5 = Fully qualified—HIRE

3.0 = Qualified—But could be convinced not to hire

2.5 = Moderately qualified—Could be convinced to hire, but probably not worth moving forward

1.0–2.0 = Underqualified—DON'T HIRE

OVERALL HIRING COMMENTS (OPTIONAL)

I ask you: Who in the actual fuck wants to fill out this form? No one. Now imagine you are a busy manager doing all your busy manager things. You may be even busier than usual because you are doing the work of the person you need to hire, which is why you need to hire someone in the first place. On top of this, after identifying ten or so candidates, after reading a hundred or so résumés, you have scheduled ten or so interviews and now have to write short essays/fill out ten or so forms about candidates you would never hire in the first place and then fight for the candidate you want to hire, not knowing if the other interviewers, people who will not have to manage and perhaps not even work with this person, feel the same way. HIRING PEOPLE IS INSANITY. Who gets hired and why they get hired are, in the end, often random—especially at a big place with lots of red tape, and maybe even more so at a small place when the boss has her head up her ass and makes arbitrary decisions. But despite all this, you can still do a few things to stack the deck in your favor.

Here's What You Can Control in an Interview

➤ Show up on time—not twenty minutes early, not five minutes late.

➤ Wear something that makes you feel great, that fits well, that doesn't do anything funny like twist or stick to itself or ride up or expose a part of your body that is perfectly fine but makes you feel self-conscious (a tattoo you don't love, an errant mole). Put this outfit on the night before and gesticulate wildly in it, bend over to pick up your phone, sit, and stand. Test-drive this outfit and see if it can pass all your awkward moves without a malfunction.

➤ Be smart and prepared enough—know a few things about the company, examples of recent company news, something you genuinely like about its mission and why you want to work there. Don't kill yourself over this.

➤ As best you can, try to be an authentic person having an authentic conversation. Don't try to be ON, which always reads as ON and doesn't let the interviewer see you for who you are.

➤ When answering questions, show that you understand the position, but don't throw around jargon just to throw around jargon and try to seem like a business bot. Most people don't say things like "KPI" and "ROI" in real life.

➤ Have one or two example of things you've done already that are relevant to the job and that you can explain in smart concise ways: "When I got to position X, it was like X, but then I spearheaded an X to make Y."

➤ Don't criticize the company—the one you're applying to, or the one you're coming from. This may seem like no-duh advice, but you'd be surprised.

➤ Don't divulge things about your life that could possibly hurt your chances of getting a job (i.e., a long commute, child-care issues, that you have no car and live with your parents two hours away). In the United States, an interviewer can't legally ask you personal questions like your age or whether you have kids or if you're coupled up. And don't disclose your problems with authority, or how you secretly hate to wake up before nine, or how cool you think it would be to knock off work at five so you can make it to your CrossFit class—all things people have told me in interviews. These small admissions tend to trip up interviewees, leaving small but lasting impressions on interviewers. When hiring people—especially when it's a difficult decision between two equally qualified candidates—nonwork details can make all the difference in the decision-making process, especially if they're not to the interviewer's taste.

➤ If it's a long interview—for more senior-level jobs, some companies like to do back-to-back interview "sprints" that can last hours, where you interview with every person on the team—practice self-care and take breaks. Speak up for what you need! Don't do that female thing of making yourself small and "not a bother" and then feel dehydrated and dizzy and desperate to pee in hour three.

➤ Always follow up within twenty-four hours, thanking your interviewer for the interview and his time.

➤ A real, live thank-you note is a perfect gesture, but it may take too much time—find out the company's timeline for making the decision. If you are going the handwritten-note path, have it pre-addressed, carry it in your bag, and write it immediately after the interview. Details from your conversation will be fresh in your mind, and if you mail it nearby, it might get there the next day.

➤ Ask questions, but not too many: three or four, max. If the person hasn't answered these yet, ask: What does success look like in this role? What are the expectations for the first six months? Asking the interviewer about a project that's made her most proud is always a nice way to shift the focus away from you for a minute, and lets you get to know the person who might be your boss.

➤ Feign at least a modicum of chill. This is probably the hardest one, but keeping your angst and anxiousness in check—not shaking your legs or twirling your hair or acting like a person who checks in about the status of a hiring decision three times a day and answers e-mails within eleven seconds of receipt—will make the interviewer more confident that you can handle the job and that you are a person with whom it would be pleasant to work. (I am telling you this, but I am the least chill person. I am an anxious foot shaker. I get so nervous in interviews that I need to keep track of my saliva production so I don't spit when I talk. I also literally return e-mails as if they are a biohazard-level contaminant, and by answering at light speed I am saving my family from death. However, none of these things get in the way of my being very good at what I do, and no one needs or wants to know any of this in the first ten minutes of meeting me.)

OK, Great, but, Really, What Should I Wear

There was a book in the 1990s called *The Rules* that taught women how to "catch a man." It was a "formula" for how to trick men into dating and dining and calling, and, especially, proposing and marrying, applying this contrived behavior to everyday life with the express goal of gaining a husband. You would not give a damn about genuine compatibility; you would not consider whether this was a partner who would love you for who you really are, who would be an equal and treat you like an equal, or, in the long run, would be a human worthy of sharing your sheets. Instead, *The Rules* told readers, Change your fundamental personality, and a man will like you. Don't talk too much. Don't call too much. Don't fuck until we say you can.

Most career guides treat getting dressed for an interview in the same way: as if looking like Career Barbie will help you catch a job, as if, by purchasing that precise, crisp blazer, you can trick someone into giving you work. This theory insults everyone and everything—you, the interviewers, work, womankind.

You should know enough about your industry to know if there is an office dress code; i.e., if it's a law or banking office that requires women to wear more conservative outfits and "hose" (DEAR GOD, HOSE), things traditionally associated

with "work clothes." But otherwise, just be yourself. Dress
like yourself—the best version of yourself, the person you
want your grandmother to see. Wear what makes you feel
confident and comfortable. Unless you love fashion and fashion magazines and you are applying for a job in fashion or
fashion magazines, don't scramble to track down $800 shoes
and a $1,500 bag. Look professional, but don't pretend to be
something you're not. I am fairly sure I have failed to get jobs
because I overthought my outfit and looked too "done"—
because I wore stiff polyester suits to an office of hoodies,
when I am not actually a stiff polyester suit person. Being in
those woman-who-goes-to-an-office outfits made me far more
uncomfortable and self-conscious and prone to nervous tics
than if I'd just pulled out a random jumpsuit and some low-
to-the-ground pumps.

I once interviewed a woman for a vice president job who
came in with no makeup, wearing a floral sundress. She looked
so relaxed and perfectly in her skin, I was immediately at ease
in her presence. We had a killer interview, she was extremely
smart, and she got the job. This is all about representing yourself in an authentic way: if you come in with Kardashian-level
glam, if you come in wearing a ramped-up, professional-lady
costume *that does not represent who you are* and the office is a
sea of athleisure and chill, you will seem like a bad fit. However, there is a limit to being your sartorial self: if you decide to
wear yoga pants and a midriff-baring top with the word NOPE
emblazoned across the front in glitter letters* to meet the president of the company where you want to work—even if this out-

---

* Actual outfit someone wore for an interview with me.

fit represents your deepest soul—you might want to rethink the message you're sending.

Instead of obsessing over the "perfect" interview outfit, give yourself extra time the morning of the interview. Smile into the mirror. Practice it all going very well. Breathe. Think of this as an adventure. Apply extra deodorant if you're afraid you smell. Bring lip balm for your chapped lips. You got this. Even if you don't, it's OK. It might wind up better anyway.

When You Don't Get the Job

I'm sorry, this sucks. Please go out and have a this-sucks party. Invite your kindest, gentlest friends, the yes women, the ones who are so nice and champion you so much that they're mostly kindly liars. You need the nice liars right now. Tomorrow you can bring in the straight shooters. Blame not getting the job on those assholes at that ridiculous company—they are stupid for not wanting you! Curse, feel mad and bad, punch things that are not people.

Somewhere in the healing-from-rejection process, remember that not getting the job often means dodging a career-killing bullet, that sometimes the VERY BEST thing that can happen is being cast off over some other sucker. I've been devastated after not landing a position I really wanted, only to find that the company went under six months later or changed direction in some gross way that would have made my heart sad and my waking life a misery.

Your natural, normal instinct when they tell you no will be to feel abject and rejected, but try to think of the job search process like the relationship search process—if they don't want you, you don't want them. That's it. If they don't want you, you don't want them. Say it over and over again. Chant it like a mantra while drinking wine out of the bottle and crying in the mirror in your underwear. Then wake up the next morning and look for the next thing. You're OK. The next thing will come. It will be better than this other thing. High-five yourself for having the courage to go for something you wanted, even if it didn't work out, even if you didn't get it. Knowing what you want is half of this crazy battle. Each rejection helps to crystallize this. You will get the next job. You will get the job that's right for you right now. And then you will have a whole new set of problems.

CHAPTER 6

Persistence, Resistance

Here's where things gets thorny, or at least thorn*ier*. This road you're walking on, this path you're trying to dig up and pave for yourself, this NEW LIFE of fulfilling work and personal destiny you are trying to live? It's not going to come easy. At least, it didn't for me. Even after you land your first job, and your second job—even after you catch a BIG break—you may do all the right things, and still, due to circumstances outside your control, it will often turn out different than you thought.

I want this story to be uplifting and inspiring. I don't want you to get fatigued by my failures. I wish I could paint a picture of me skipping around Manhattan to my first job, wearing a good skirt with good hair and carrying a colorful umbrella, all pluck, adorable quirks, and Aaron Sork–ian early-professional delight. But more than any smiley cliché of what career success looks like, I want you to know that it's totally OK and normal if your early road to success never feels easy—that "putting

yourself out there" is not some magic bullet for quickly making
dreams come true. I want you to know that the thrill you
feel being on the path to your dream is not mutually exclusive
from the feeling of discomfort, and, on occasion, misery.

Finding career success is tumultuous and labyrinthine. It's a
continuum; it's unexpected and odd. It will hurt, and sometimes
it will bring you down. Your vulnerable networking e-mails will
go unanswered. You may feel unlucky. You will call your mother
and cry. You will make bad decisions and accidentally find yourself in unpleasant circumstances. Failing repeatedly or having
the world fail you, working jobs that make you feel abject and
lost, feeling out of place and even completely fucked—none of
this precludes your getting what you want. It's just part of the
process. Your so-called mistakes hold the same value as your so-
called wins. The secret to "making it" is not some elusive magical thinking or a set of keys that only the rich, intellectually
elite, or even supremely talented are handed the day they are
born. The secret to becoming successful is little more than re-
silience, smarts, and the capacity to keep going when the world
tells you to fuck off. The power you have is that when you get
plowed down, you can pick yourself up again. You can believe
in your ambitions and your potential. You don't need to dwell on
feeling like a loser, a burnt turd on the bottom of a shoe. You
can believe that you are unique and worthy and have something
to offer, that you deserve to be here, that this is a long game that
you can and eventually will win, even if it doesn't feel that way
right now.

This belief will sometimes stand in stark contrast with what
the universe is telling you. Sometimes it will stand in oppo-

sition to "signs," or what your horoscope, or a fortune cookie, or a psychic you gave too much money to on the street, And rarely will it look like it does in movies or sound like I MADE IT! anecdotes on your favorite podcast. Sometimes it's all more depressing and mundane—and even then, you shouldn't give up. Destiny is not a GPS stem that turns on the minute you start doing the right thin and tells you exactly where to go. You have to accept uncertai and the scariness of the unknown. You have to keep mov mewhere, one foot in front of the other, to give yourself hat it will be better than it was before. I didn't give up be I was touched by an angel or had some sixth sense that it ll going to work out. I remained dogged and determined e I had nowhere else to turn. I made the life I wanted de he world telling me I wouldn't, multiple times.

And it all kind of sucked until it did not.

When I finally got to New Yor York rejected me. Remember that first job I got at *Ins* ell, I lost it six months after I found it. After all those mo d all those twenty-four interviews, six months into the e company went under. The news was devastating, mad se by the fact that *Inside* was a perfect first job, the kind happens so rarely—the kind where the stars and the hur s and the newness of the company all align to make som g thrilling, hopeful, and special, something that everyon excited to be working on and around. I did not anticipat lemise. One day we were doing all the work—bustling wi deas, collaborating, reporting, writing, cheering each othe all the smart people doing all the smart things they shou nd then it was over, in a private HR sit-down in the blue-tube conference room: *Here's your severance package. Here's that thing about Cobra you'll never read. Here's the unemployment information you'll fish out from the bottom of your bag when you run out of money in 3.5 weeks.*

On the last day, when I was packing up my tchotchkes, stashing my free office supplies, and wiping away tears, my boss, Richard, pulled me aside. "I want you to know that most of your jobs are not going to feel like this, not going to be this special," he said. "Most of your jobs are just going to feel like jobs that you have to do to get paid. You get maybe two or three of these in your entire career."

I nodded. I thanked him. At the time I took it all as kindly, if cynical, Dad advice.

I did not know how right he would be.

Turns Out, I'm a Terrible Secretary

After *Inside* went under, through the connections I'd made there, I was offered a role as assistant to the editor in chief of a troubled yet self-important magazine in a sterile Midtown Manhattan building in an office strewn with vintage typewriters on pedestals under spotlights, a subtle WE ARE WRITERS aesthetic choice. Though it was 2001, there was a throwback 1980s vibe to the place—a #tbt of understated misogyny, men in suspenders, cans of Tab in the employee fridge.

My new boss was regimented. He woke every morning at 5:30 a.m., had one of those Very Productive People/Secrets of Success agendas from 5:30 to 6:30, when he ate a teaspoon of skim milk and two almonds and did 280 crunches and rubbed

the *New Yorker* all over his body* before he lint-brushed his entire life. This boss, let's call him Rafe, loved New York power
and New York power players and being known and in the
know. As a boss (in this particular role, at this particular time),
he contained three modes: nervous, spazzing, yelling.† Rafe
expected a traditional boss/secretary relationship: I should arrive at 8:30 a.m., unlock his office, turn on the lights, open the
blinds, fluff his pillows, have his coffee waiting. I should stock
his office mini fridge with two Diet Coke cans and four seltzer
waters. If I did not keep the fridge stocked in just this way at all
times, he would yell my name over and over—"Jennifer! Jennifer! Jennifer!"—even though I was sitting outside his door, just
a few feet away. When I entered the office, I would find him
waiting at his desk, not looking up, arm extended to point at
the open-doored fridge.

Between 8:50 and 9:00 a.m., Rafe would arrive at the office,
and by 9:03 we would have our first "status" meeting of the
day. He would hand me his to-do list; I should make sure it
was done. I answered his phone. I ordered his private cars. I
arranged and scheduled his lunches and breakfasts and drinks
meetings and kept his calendar. I ordered flowers for women

---

* Not really. He did not rub down his body with *New Yorker* magazines.

† Throughout my career, I've witnessed this pathology: some people,
as soon as they gain even a glimmer of power, become dismissive and
cruel to underlings, as if the office were a space where they felt free to
let their inner creep loose—screaming, demanding, crying, behaving in
ways that are childish and unreasonable because they know their assistants have no recourse but to endure the abuse. These same people can
be warm and gregarious in the rest of their lives, and charm the business slacks off anyone they deem "important." A true mark of a person's
goodness and integrity is how she treats her assistants—and waiters.
End rant.

he wanted to professionally woo. From just the right florist. With just the right arrangement. If I failed to do this, he ranted until his face became mottled, a Rorschach test of splotchy magenta. I found and sent out-of-print books to famous writers and editors to whom Rafe was sucking up. I typed his letters. If he wasn't in the office when I typed them, if he dictated them over the phone, I wrote "Dictated but not read" at the bottom. I stayed until he left every night, sometimes long into it. When I asked if I could leave early one Friday afternoon to attend my brother's high school graduation, I was told no. What if he needed me?

In the interest of not leaning too hard into a victim narrative here—because this work was not tarring roofs or digging ditches, and also because nothing is that simple, even when our brains want it to be—I was not stellar at this work. I made clumsy mistakes on things like expenses. I forgot critical things like appointments. I was sold a position that would be half learning the magazine ropes and half administrative, but when I arrived, it turned out that the math was entirely off; instead I was taking beverage orders and notes and opening blinds and doing little else. Rafe and I were a disastrously bad fit, something I should have spotted right away. If I'd known then what I know now, I would have asked more questions in the interview. I was too focused on just *getting the job*, and not enough on whether it was a job I could actually do. I did not possess the disposition for a role like this. I was too disorganized, too spiritually old; I wanted too much, too fast. Most important, I was fundamentally uninterested in what my employer had to offer: very little nuts-and-bolts teaching, and a sycophantic, who-you-know style of working in which I would never excel. These are the things you learn. This is how you eventually make better decisions.

In what was becoming a pattern, the magazine where Rafe and I worked together folded four months later. Rafe went on to fancy roles doing fancy things. There was no love lost between us. Years later, when my name came up at a party in front of a mutual friend, Rafe sneered, "She's so American." We were both Americans, of course. We were just from different Americas.

The Busboy of Magazines

Next came the finale in my initial New York trifecta of failure. Through another *Inside* connection, I was hired as a fact-checker at a glamorous-extravagant general-interest magazine that held its glamorous-extravagant 1,000-person launch party at a major New York landmark and, after blowing through tens of millions of dollars, closed two years later, marking the end of new glamorous-extravagant general-interest magazines for good. But I'm getting ahead of myself.

Though fact-checking is still a relevant, important job at prestigious publications, in the digital era it almost seems quaint, like it was from the stone tablet era, or a time when we wrote accurate things in sand. Until a few years ago, fact-checking was an in-demand skill, a magazine job that could be learned quickly and was a step up from getting editors coffee. Most companies gussied up the position as "researcher/

reporter," but while fact-checkers did provide additional reporting for writers, you were rarely given any credit.

Fact-checkers are the people paid to annoy everyone at magazines: they delay publication of stories while they're trying to
confirm facts, they question every sentence of a writer's reporting, and when they catch mistakes, both minor and egregious,
they have to bring them to the attention of people more senior than they are, often big writers and big editors, sometimes
with big egos. Seemingly insignificant edits made in haste can
change the entire meaning of a story; sources are often full of it
and, pressed a second time, contradict what they said the first;
and "general knowledge" facts are often just plain wrong. Fact-
checking is a tedious, necessary, sometimes politically messy
job, which varies depending on the integrity of the writer and
the editor. Fact-checkers are often left to clean up sloppy reporting and ensuing editorial chaos. Editors and writers need you,
but they don't necessarily respect you. You complete a lot of the
grunt work, but get none of the glory. When I tried to explain
what I was doing to an old restaurant friend, he deduced, "So
you're kind of the busboy of the magazine." Not a perfect metaphor, but close.

The first story I fact-checked was on Chandra Levy, the DC
intern who was found murdered, but who had also had an affair with a married congressman named Gary Condit. Her
killer was still at large. The piece was 12,000 words, and filled
with all sorts of salacious and potentially litigious allegations.
I had never fact-checked anything before. I had a week to verify every fact in the story, from the correct spelling of people's
and towns' names to finding concrete sources for factual leaps.
On my first day of work, I met with the staff lawyer to wade

through anything she deemed problematic and potentially litigious. She had dozens of pages of notes.

The writer wanted all of the allegations kept in. The editor
made promises I did not know if we could keep. On the second
day, I had to call Levy's mom to verify facts and quotes I could
not find elsewhere. She was polite, but then started quietly
crying and had to take a break from the call. It was all bone-
crushingly sad, my first reminder of the weight of the job—that
there were real humans on the other side of these transcripts,
that this was not some fantasy role I'd concocted in a dream,
that I was not a supporting character in that David Spade sitcom. I was in over my head, I knew it, and I asked for help—
which is what you should do if ever a scandalous 12,000-word
true-crime manuscript is plopped on your desk, and you have
little idea how to handle it, or anytime you feel underwater at
a new job. If I had done it alone, I would have failed. I solicited
above-the-call-of-duty aid from the lawyer and support from
my coworkers. Whenever I was in doubt, I asked. We used careful language to couch rumors, to make them legally safe. The
facts were solid enough; all the names were spelled correctly. It
felt like we'd violated something, but no one sued. This would
become my measure of success.

Fact-checking was often done in the eleventh hour, late at
night, just before sending the pages to printers. It was a time
when people were stressed out and even strung out, and no
one was at their best. Arguments ensued. I once fought with a
famous editor at midnight over a profile of Dan Rather. Facts
had been fudged in the editing process to make the bland story
about a septuagenarian news anchor "sexier." I remember
saying too loudly, "I'm sorry! We can't make him sexy!" and

walking away, later afraid I'd lose my job. Another night, after dismantling a well-regarded journalist's reporting on a shaky feature about a pop diva's breakdown, I spent a tense hour in the editor's office with the writer on speakerphone, going line by line, fact by fact, gripping the edges of my seat, wishing for my death. On unverifiable information, the writer's defense was "Oh, everyone knows that," or "Come on, that's *out there* already." I liked the writer, I admired her, I wanted to be her. At the very least, I desperately wanted her to think I was cool. Instead, because my job was Annoying Fact Person, I insisted that without sourcing we could not consider something true, even if the "not-true" things were the linchpin of the story. The editor was left to decide between us. I hated being this person, hated asserting myself in this way, calling out my heroes for their mistakes.

But it didn't matter if I hated it or not, if I could get comfortable within this position of nonauthority authority or parlay it into something else: the glamorous-extravagant general-interest magazine was shuttered one frigid night in January, five months after I'd arrived. We heard the news whispered for days before, hinted at and spoken around, the way information is conveyed to kids who grown-ups deem unfit to know the truth. When it finally happened, we huddled together in the bullpen of our airy Chelsea office as the famous, all-black-clad New York media figures who ran/owned/were forever aligned with the place took turns announcing our bleak fate. Cheap champagne was poured into cheap plastic cups. We stayed together, drinking and packing, long into the night, as we were told to. Reporters were waiting outside for a statement. Everyone wanted to know why we'd failed. I was too green and naive to understand the fascination or most of the fuss. I only knew that I was out of a job, again.

Every Day I'm Side Hustlin'

New York knocked me around quite a bit. There was nothing about my first two years as a professional in the city that suggested I should stay in the city as a professional. Not the publishing downturn and recession I'd entered into, not the collapse of my first three places of employment, not the subsequent weeks-long lapses of income, not falling into debt, not being constantly broke and often alone. Not my increasingly random living situations in oddly configured apartments in Brooklyn, an hour away from work. Not the room I rented that was so small I had to lift my futon mattress to open my dresser drawers. Not the room after that, in the apartment with the slumlord roommate who owned the lease, whose actual day job was professional clown, who decided it would be fun to start hiding inappropriate objects in my bed. Not my junkyard dating life, not my increased reliance on alcohol and drugs to get me through the week, to mask social anxiety and my fear that I was an impostor who should call it a day and go home.

I wouldn't find another full-time job in publishing for two years. I had a paltry severance and scant unemployment benefits, but I was already in the hole, my credit cards maxed.[*] I'd sold everything I could sell—my books and CDs, even my

[*] And by "credit cards," I mean rectangles of plastic with a choose-your-own design like Tweety Bird or the American flag and a limit of $500, minus an $89.95 annual fee, with a 68.8 percent interest rate.

quarter-carat De Beers engagement ring. There was no new cash valve to tap.

In a vulnerable, self-doubting moment I considered going back to waitressing. I went as far as to set up an interview at a pricey downtown NYC landmark restaurant, a place where, because of a well-connected friend, I was pretty much a shoo-in, where I would've made more money than magazine fact-checking and assisting combined. On the way to that interview, on the subway from Brooklyn, restaurant résumé printed and in my purse, I got train-sick, a combination of nausea and panic, claustrophobia and cold sweat. If I didn't exit the car immediately, I was sure I would check off number four on my list of worst New York nightmares* and *vomit on the train.*

I managed to exit the car and get out of the tunnel, up the stairs into the cool almost-spring air. I missed the next train. I missed my interview. Instead, I walked long and far, around the edges of misty Brooklyn, by the river, looking over the city. I didn't want to wait tables anymore. I was nearly thirty years old; I knew that if I didn't fully commit to my dream now, if I didn't focus and try to finish what I'd started, fight through the unpleasantness of setbacks and downturns and just plain dumb luck and keep going, I might never have the nerve to try again.

I now had fact-checking as a skill, and I capitalized on it. In the early '00s, magazines hired fact-checkers on a project basis. You could pick up work for a week or two a month, when they filed the most stories and needed extra help. Using all the connections I'd made at the three jobs I'd lost, I landed freelance

---

* First three: 1. Pushed onto subway tracks; 2. Rat in toilet; 3. Victim of guy who throws feces.

fact-checking gigs, bouncing from magazine to magazine, checking facts and learning a lot about the inner workings of each place and the business itself as I went. When each assignment ended, I had to hustle for the next, but eventually I had a steady flow, a roster of publications that would ask me back, a semblance of regular income, though it was not enough and could all go away at any time.

The majority of my work during these years was in women's magazines, calling up (suspiciously, uniformly) svelte, attractive white women and making sure they'd actually said the things we were printing in their woman-on-the-street interviews (they often hadn't), or talking to celebrity stylists, trainers, or chefs about their clients' routines. Did JLo do fifty squats a day or a hundred? Was Jessica Simpson's fave hair product leave-in conditioner or hair serum? Was Britney's new perfume meant to smell like fruit or wood or something called tuberose? The rest was standard-issue ladyland topics: trends of the season everyone should be wearing, foods to make you lose weight now, tricks to make you live better, smell better, fuck better, be the best version of you, the clone of everyone else.

The job required awkward cold-calling and a good deal of on-the-phone time, which meant I had zero choice but to stop sounding like a panicked, overly formal child every time I had to ring someone up. As a fact-checker I scoured interview transcripts and re-interviewed sources constantly. I learned new ways to research every day. It was a dead-end job—fact-checkers rarely became editors, I was told time and again by various people in HR—and not what I wanted to do forever, but there was real value in it that I could not have seen if I'd rejected it, thinking it was below me. Fact-checking taught me how writers found and pulled stories together. It taught me how stories fell apart and what you needed to keep them from getting killed. I didn't know it at the time, but it was critical to building my confidence and expanding my skills. It made me a better and more versatile editor and writer. But it was not without its indignities.

Toward the end of my years as a fact-checker, I worked at a sexy-lady magazine that, at the time, was loose with the facts, a place that hired fact-checkers not to maintain editorial integrity but mainly as a safeguard against getting sued. I checked facts on penises and nipples and how to touch penises and nipples. I checked facts on buttholes and bleaching buttholes and safe ways and not-so-safe ways to insert things inside buttholes. I verified information on phrases and words I would never say in public but now had to say regularly to strangers over the phone, with a straight face, in an official capacity. I once had to call a source quoted in a story on queefing, and referenced as an expert on the subject. When I reached her, she said, "Oh. My. God. It must be so embarrassing for you to have a job where you call and ask people questions like this!" I did not mention that she was about to be in print as the expert on queefs.

Fact-checking became my pay-the-bills day job, but I worked nights too. During the day I was paying for my present survival, but after I went home, I was working for my future. I wrote stories and pitched them everywhere I could, regularly pulling all-nighters, side-hustling hard. I turned my nose up at nothing. I wrote for special advertising sections. I took assignments from Target's short-lived in-house magazine, writing, inexplicably, about a man who built Hollywood's pyrotechnic displays. I created quizzes for a little-known bathroom and kitchen magazine, the one less popular than the leader in the space—*Find your unique bathroom style! What's your countertop personality? The right faucet for you? Take our quiz!* I was professional, I turned assignments in on time and at the requested length, and I never turned anything down. Every single piece made me a better writer and broadened my network; every single connection led me to something else. It was slow, methodical work, building something from nothing. It required a great deal of humility and persistence. It took me two full years to get anywhere near decent pay and a proper byline. But once I did, I never stopped.

In the past few years, we've fetishized and romanticized the idea of a "side hustle," to a point that it's almost cute, like a hobby, like you're painting watercolors in the park with your book group after an afternoon tea (#goals!). But for some of us, side hustles aren't an adorable social media affectation; they are a necessity, vital to our survival, a way to catch up to our peers if we're behind, to work toward what we really want, to fulfill our dreams while still paying our rent during the day.

Unless you are independently wealthy or the recipient of some sweet nepotism or both, in these early years of your career, working extra hours, keeping your professional irons in multiple fires, *working*, not just *playing*, at the side hustle, is the only strategy I know to get through a tight job market and keep yourself on a path to success. This is especially true if you're lacking a conventional pedigree, you're an odd fit and don't look/sound/seem like the rest, and you're trying to break into a competitive and/or creative field. At night and on weekends, take classes, go to networking events, seek out online professional communities and private e-mail, Facebook, and

Slack groups. Lean on each and every one of your connections; gain experience wherever and whenever you can. This process does not have to be demoralizing. You might be broke, but you're free. Your career is a scavenger hunt and an adventure. Follow what interests you; say yes to everything that seems intriguing. This time is about you—not your parents, not your future partners or potential children. It's about being nimble, discovering and getting what you want, and investing in your future. This period of your career may feel exhausting, but if you keep going, if you stay hopeful and don't stagnate, it can also be exhilarating.

The more relevant the work you do during the day, the more connected you can make your professional worlds, the better. Think creatively. Is there a part of your business that is easier to break into than others? Is there a skill you can exploit or a side door you haven't explored? Is there a respected local nonprofit with work relevant to your field, where you can volunteer and gain a good résumé line? Does a company you like need help seasonally, or on weekends or nights? Look at the LinkedIn profiles of people whose careers you want. What and where were their first jobs? Reach out for information interviews. Keep your request concise and clear: Can I ask you three questions about your career? Eventually, if you stay focused and think strategically, if you take it step by step and bit by bit, you can force your paying-the-bills work and the work you love to merge. Eventually, you will catch a break. Eventually you will control the chaos, and this will all feel less crazy.

After two years working essentially two full-time jobs, I got my break in the most clichéd, obvious way: I started writing about what I knew. For the moment, New York's fickle heart had alighted upon yoga and yogis. Buddhism was in vogue; interest in neo-hippie culture and all things faintly Eastern surged. There were few mainstream writers who took the trend seriously, who knew the lingo and players in the space, who could toe the line between healthy skepticism and respectful understanding of what these therapies and practices meant to people's lives. I'd grown up around alternative medicine and New Ageism, around sage burning, acupuncture, homeopathics, health-food coops, drum circles, sweat-lodge ceremonies, past-life regression. My mother practiced reiki and shiatsu massage out of our home; my dad meditated silently for ten days a year; my therapist in high school, chosen by my parents, punctuated sessions in her all-pink office with crystals and incense to help me "heal." When a local New York magazine launched a section on "chilling out," on Manhattan yoga classes and meditation centers and all things spas, I pitched them more than a dozen ideas. They accepted six. I thought I'd come to New York to write about *serious* things for *serious* places. Like everyone else, I'd dreamed of my byline in "Talk of the Town" font. Instead, I pivoted and found my voice by beginning to own a beat where there wasn't a lot of competition, where I could carve out a space of my own. I wrote about dental spas and sensory deprivation tanks; I got colonics and EMDR therapy and chest facials (chestals?). When I stripped down for the city's most expensive massage, the masseuse lifted the 20,000-thread-count sheet covering my nude form and asked, "Do you run?" Then: "You should." I wrote it all down.

When a full-time, on-staff-with-benefits Chill Out editor position opened up a few months later, I applied. I had no editing experience, and I did not get the job. But they remembered me.

A few weeks later, when their first-choice candidate flamed out, the magazine called again. In our interview, the boss said he was dubious about my lack of experience, but I had a good reputation and an "air of competence." He was willing to take a risk. The job was mine.

Before I left, I thanked him profusely. I shook his hand too hard and for too long. I turned in my visitor's pass to the receptionist, and I screamed in the elevator. I jumped up and down. I bounced out of the building of my soon-to-be first job as an editor full-face grinning, heart so full of accomplishment joy I nearly burst.

CHAPTER 7

Surviving Yourself

Landing the Chill Out editor job was the first time I felt real. I was a legitimate professional—I had the business cards to prove it. I had a seat at the table now. Instead of chasing and running and running and chasing like I'd done for the previous seven years, I could catch my breath for a minute and get acclimated to my surroundings. I could sort out who I was and what I could do in Official Officeland.

It's safe to assume, if you picked up this book and you've read this far, that, like me, you often feel like a skinless chicken running around this world. You might be physically or socially awkward; innocuous situations might trip you up, like what to do with your hands when you're talking or how to say good-bye to your boss at the end of the day. Maybe you laugh at these situations with friends, you joke about how you were born with these strange doll limbs that don't work on command. Maybe you make a lot of jokes about yourself. It's funny but not funny ha ha. Sometimes it feels like too much just to be in your brain—you absorb the tiniest details, the ones that pass others by; they stick with you. You wonder about the smallest change in your boss's expression and obsess over what an errant exclamation point on a work e-mail really means.

Maybe you're ambitious but you're not an operator, a schmoozer, or a natural-born faker. You may be shy or an "extroverted introvert" or even a "go-getter," but you're not what someone would call "slick." You've watched those people, the effortless self-promoters, the shameless movers and shakers who seem to ask for and get what they want from the world with ease. You admire them, you observe their power like you would a cheetah or a moon landing or Beyoncé in the first five songs of *Lemonade*. You wish you could take their assertive parts and leave behind the parts that make you want to soak your soul in a salt bath. Sometimes, too often, you feel apologetic just for being you, in your skin. You overanalyze situations to a paralyzing degree. But you're getting better. You're trying to own your space on this planet. There's a glimmer inside you, an ember that says you are not just good but great, that knows you belong, that wants not only to compete but also to win. You fan that flame inside cautiously, optimistically, quietly. You don't joke about this. Maybe much of working life and the professional world still seems gobsmacking, inorganic, insane. But you're trying to normalize it all, to make a confident home out of your body.

To do this, you'll need to soothe the self-hating, self-sabotaging parts of your brain. You'll need to shut down—or at least *slow down*—the overthinking and self-consciousness that lead you to false conclusions, the paralyzing insecurity and inappropriate attention grabs. You need to survive yourself.

Let me walk you through this.

Office Life Might Not Live
Up to Your Dreams

When I was in college, failing out for the second time, I wrote a paper on *The Great Gatsby*. Like all my work in those days, it was a half-assed rush job, finished late the night before it was due. My theme was trite and obvious, something like *"The Great Gatsby* and the American Dream Blah Blah—a double-spaced, exactly-to-length-and-not-one-sentence-more piece of perfunctory horseshit by Jennifer Romolini." The only reason that I remember this paper is because of something I put in the bibliography, a piece of criticism from an academic I cannot name now, and probably couldn't have named ten minutes after I turned the paper in. In it was a line referring to Gatsby's ambition and ultimate demise that has stuck with me ever since: "The dream was not worthy of the dreamer."

When I finally got up the nerve to pursue a job in publishing, I had visions of how smart, glamorous, exciting, and sexy it would be, like Bob Woodward and Carl Bernstein combined with a dash of Drew Barrymore, and Kate Hudson's best '90s movies tossed in. But, especially in those early, dues-paying years, that vision could not have been further from the reality. The work culture did not live up to my expectations. Bosses often behaved like oversize children. Gossip and petty grievances were rampant between coworkers, who seemed to behave more like high schoolers or even grade schoolers than the sophisticated urban professionals I'd expected. Work environments were sterile and ugly. Most of the work was mundane. The dream was not worthy of the fantasy I'd projected upon it. It rarely would be.

Some people seem to really get into office life, arriving each morning with a thermos full of hope and artisanal coffee. Others strut in with their best Sun Tzu posture, swaggering and ready to fight. But if you are a sensitive, skeptical human, you may have a visceral reaction to the unnaturalness of your workspace the first time you walk in, and instead of storming the gate to success, you may wish to recoil. You may also feel this in your first conversation with a stiff corporate entity like HR. You may marvel at the dreariness of office furnishings and Excel spreadsheets and wonder how people can keep saying "Let's take this offline" and talking about "low-hanging fruit" and still be actual humans. At the work holiday party, you will make a joke that no one gets. Then, finally, about six weeks in—when someone is complaining about how someone else switched the vending machine offerings, maybe starting an indignant e-mail chain about this with a deadly serious subject line—suddenly, no matter what you are doing, how grateful you are to be doing it, or how much you really want this job to work out, you will look around and think, Is this what I went through all that shit for? HOW CAN THIS BE HAPPENING?

When you have this feeling, when you feel crushed under all the *The Office*–ness, don't dwell on it. Take a step back, acknowledge all of the foibles and silly formality of this world, but DO NOT allow it to trigger an identity crisis. You are not your soulless cube or your coveted office supplies, and you are certainly not your dumb struggles with the office scanner or your unfinished, overdue HR training on "respect." You are not going to die of corporateness. This is simply the work you need to endure to do the work you want. This situation is not permanent. You are building the foundation of a career. You worked too hard to get here to let it go because some business-y bullshit bums you out. If you focus on becoming great at what you do (which we will talk about more specifically later in this book, and which I heartily encourage), if you keep your mind open to learning and seek out new challenges and opportunities and are kind to people in the process, no one and nothing can slow you down—especially not something as frivolous as the corporate-culture nonsense conducted under those fluorescent lights. And, sure, your first jobs may not always be worthy of you and your dreams, but your big-picture goals and career certainly are.

Small Talk When You Like Big Talk

Small talk is not the worst thing that human beings have ever burdened themselves with voluntarily. That prize probably falls to duvet covers or comments sections or the entirety of Election 2016. But as a social construct, small talk is silly; it's a quagmire, a labyrinth of falseness that we've all forced ourselves to endure to establish "rapport." It's someone asking you questions about topics they don't care about, and listening to answers they don't want to hear. It's a balloon of empty, air-filling words passed back and forth until an interruption saves you or the conversation dominant decides it's OK to stop.

Small talk is especially paralyzing to those of us who, left to our own devices, would only ever engage in big talk; who are compulsively confessional; who must announce, when sad or stoned, that we are sad or stoned, because holding these facts inside our bodies might kill us, even though no one else would have guessed. In my personal life, I prefer intense, intimate, deranged, nonlinear talk. I like knowing how people really feel about things. Anything else makes me feel cagey and strange, like we're living in the Upside-Down, like I am acting in a play called *Ha Ha Ha How's the Weather? It's Obvious You Are Not Yourself Right Now.* But this is not everyone's conversational preference, and over the years, I've learned it's a little much to expect heart-to-hearts with strangers over cookies and/or the copy machine.

I'm not going to put on some rah-rah posture and tell you that small talk is great (!) once you've mastered it (!). I'm not here to convince you that something awkward is actually wonderful if only you could learn these tricks and change. But small talk needs to happen in your career and in your life, especially when you are building a network or starting a new job or talking to your landlord or communicating for the first time with just about any adult,* at any time. Here's how to "kind of" do it.

The best way to engage in small talk is to maintain some version of yourself throughout. Acting like an obsequious phony will only result in a desire to drown yourself in the nearest sink, a sensation we want to avoid, obviously. Ask yourself what type of small talk is tolerable to you. Do you like to talk about books or TV or food or bracelets? Can you actually discuss the weather and not combust? Make the commitment to engage with the human before you and then be curious. Recognize that everyone has at least one interesting thing to tell

---

* Not children. Children give less of a fuck about small talk than anyone on the planet and would rather talk about real shit like dessert or butts or what's in space because children are the best.

you, and ask questions. When you're at work, ask about stuff in people's office cubes that seem conversation-worthy. Ask about their new dogs and new clogs. When in doubt, say what you're thinking but are afraid to say because you think it will be too dumb, remembering the basic truth about small talk: nothing is too dumb. Ask if your eyeliner looks like spiders, or how the person you're talking to applied hers so well today. Bring up factual oddities: ask your coworker if she too has noticed how every single thing in the office is the same muted shade of gray. Ask if she likes the frosting on these cupcakes in this month's conference-room birthday party or if she liked the other cupcake frosting better. Talk about places to get bomb cupcakes. When relevant, offer up something of yourself, like your obsession with John Stamos or how you are currently binge-watching the entire six-season arc of *The West Wing* or found the best Etsy store for vintage saltshakers. Conversation will wax and wane; it will not always go well. You will feel anxious. It's OK. You're doing this on your terms. You may go weird, but you don't have to go home.

One strategy I've tried with small talk at work that has brought me from totally sucking at it to being kind of OK is, I started giving genuine compliments whenever I felt them. And not just about someone's dress or shoes or new hair. I started telling people when their professional efforts had real value, when they had an awesome idea or pulled off a project in an excellent way. Real, you-feel-them compliments go a long way; they take you out of your awkwardness and into genuine connection; they make people feel validated and good. They diffuse the tension and inherent competitive vibes that happen in professional situations. Whatever strategy you implement as you're learning small talk: Stay positive. Be friendly and kind. Don't become the person who bitches about work all the time. Everyone learns to hate that person, and eventually, you will hate yourself too.

Networking for Haters

Hi, would you like to stand around a crowded, slightly under-air-conditioned room talking to strangers while clutching a flat seltzer or a glass of buttered tannins being passed off as wine?

No? Well, too bad, because sometimes you must. Sometimes this is the only way you'll gain continued access to your career.

Life would be the best if we could make all of our professional connections in natural, normal, authentic ways. Like if you were hanging out getting your fro-yo one night, and the woman in line behind you got the same weird gummy-balls topping and then the two of you laughed—"What are these gummy balls, anyway? Ha ha"—and then you admired each other's fanny packs, and after laughing and admiring, she said, "By the way, I am the president of a cool company in your field, here's my card, call me about life opportunities and we'll get more fro-yo for real."

Unfortunately for us mortals, career-making meet-cutes rarely, if ever, happen. Usually we meet the people who will have professional meaning in our lives in more contrived, stultifying ways: by stalking potential connections on social media, sliding into their DMs with awkward requests, "liking" almost everything they do. At events, lectures, conferences, work parties, panel talks. When they roll through our companies for a "lunch." Through another connection, then out at an initially awkward coffee meeting, like a vocational blind date.

Networking is small talk with a mission. The key to being successful at it is to approach it strategically: Do your homework on potential mentors and professional allies before you meet them, virtually or IRL. Find your commonalities—we went to the same school! We know the same lady! *We both have dogs OMG.* Compliment them about specific parts of their careers or projects you particularly admired. In person, own that you know them "from the Internet," and steer into your Google searching and your social media fangirling. Say that you follow them on Twitter, that you love their Snaps. It's OK, it's expected, it's what we all do. Networking is actually easier than day-to-day conversation because the power dynamics are set: people love to talk about themselves, and most people love to give advice. Just make sure to read social cues and put appropriate boundaries around the interaction: Is this a vice president and you are an assistant and they have lots of other people to talk to at this event? Keep your comments brief. Are you talking to an author you love, and she seems not busy and genuinely interested in what you're discussing? Ask her everything. Is the conversation online? Ask three pertinent questions. Don't overtly stalk someone everywhere you can find her. Be spacious and gracious. Get what you need from your networking mark, and don't get greedy with her time.

The most important part of networking: Establish a casual plan for follow-up—"Is it OK to e-mail you?"—and, if you're in person, always get a business card. Even if you throw it away later, even if someone had to fish through her purse for them and the two of you stood together for longer than a cool amount of time. Should you need it later, you want that direct line of connection. You want to be able to say "We met at that . . . Thanks for giving me your card. . . . I have a follow-up . . ."

If you don't get a business card, connect on LinkedIn within twenty-four hours of meeting someone. Maybe that sentence made you think, "OMG, not LinkedIn, kill me. LinkedIn is so basic." But I am here to tell you that in 2017, LinkedIn is a necessary basic. Bosses use it, recruiters use it, all kinds of other people who have been tasked to find people for jobs use it. So, seriously, type up a smart but not over-the-top résumé for LinkedIn and upload a photo of yourself that looks like you and not like drunk-you-at-the-pool-with-your-cut-off-arm-around-drunk-bestie. And generally, even if something like LinkedIn is not "cool," necessarily, it's a networking tool. You want all the tools you can have in your toolbox, coolness factor be damned.

Meetings Give Me Hives

Boiled down to its essence, here is a challenge you will probably face most often at work: HOW DO I SEEM NORMAL IN THIS SITUATION and PLEASE DON'T LET THEM KNOW I'M WEIRD. This is especially true of meetings, the first time in our lives when we are paid to be penned in airless, confined spaces, propped around spaceship-like tables and forced to converse with other people in ways that don't initially make sense.

A lot of things in offices are total nonsense, but having insightful, creative, and constructive things to say in meetings is, in many or most industries, critical to your success. Sure, you can mess up a few, but as a long-term strategy, meetings are a moment to showcase your value and collaborate with your coworkers in front of people who make decisions about your paycheck. They're also a moment when your boss gets to see the seeds of your leadership skills; the way you solve problems and think on your feet. Meetings are a giant pain in the ass, of course. They steal time away from actual work and fun non-work and are filled with all kinds of inside jokes and fraught interpersonal dynamics, hidden social rules, and secret corporate etiquette, plus pressure on everyone to perform. It's enough to make anyone feel panicked and edgy. It's enough to make us weirdos implode.

If you're uncomfortable in meetings, anticipate the problem and come up with a plan that makes you feel strong and safe. For example, talking in meetings used to make me literally break out in neck hives. I was really insecure, and because my impostor-syndrome dial was always turned up high, I didn't like people looking at me, and I worried that the things I had to say sounded dumb. But I knew meetings were important. After more than a few awkward, red-faced meeting performances, I began type-A prepping for them. I overprepared answers to questions I might be asked and ideas I might need to present. I wrote notes about exactly what I wanted to say before I had to say it. These notes were sometimes just an outline of the points I wanted to hit, but if I was feeling really nervous, I'd write out a full script, including where to say "and," "but," and "the." When it was my turn to present, I consulted my scripts, which were in my notebook. By bringing these "notes," I made it appear to bosses that I truly gave a damn about their meeting, and I was able to say everything I needed to say while remaining calm. Everybody won.

Here are the basic rules of meetings—follow them, and you'll be fine. Don't be late. Don't look at your phone. Don't talk just to talk. Be a little extra cheerful and grateful. If you're not quite sure, keep your comments brief and neutral. Say things like "That sounds right" and "Thank you!" If you don't know an answer, don't make it up, but don't say no either. Instead, say something like "I will get that to you by the end of the day," or "Let me double-check my information and e-mail you right after this." Later, as you work into more senior roles, have bullet points you want to cover, ideas you'd like to pitch, facts about projects you want to make sure get heard. Say them when it's your turn to talk, and fight to make sure you do get a turn to talk. Speak up in every open call for ideas. After about a dozen or so meetings, you will start to feel less anxious. Probably you'll just feel kind of numb and bored, like everyone else.

Last thought on meetings—and this is super-important to realize as you enter more and more business situations—no matter how heart-thumpingly anxious you feel, no one knows how weird it feels inside your head. As long as you don't say "Let's burn this motherfucker down!" or run through the room wearing zero pants, no one is noticing all your weird quirks. Everyone is distracted by their own stuff. They want to get out of the meeting as badly as you do, and they're thinking about their next meeting and how they're going to kick ass so hard, or when they can pick up their "Telltale Heart"–beating phones, or what exciting or unexciting thing they are going to get for lunch. They're not worrying about whether you're weird. And if they are, honestly, it's their problem, not yours.

Getting "in Trouble"

Here's what's going to happen. You are going to make mistakes. You are going to "reply all" to an e-mail when you meant to reply to one. In this e-mail, you will say something that is not quite a fireable offense, but something mean-spirited and embarrassing as fuck. You are going to get caught sorting through four hundred pairs of shoes on Zappos when you should be sorting through four hundred files your boss sent you, files that were due yesterday. You will show up to work forgetting it's the day the company president is in town, wearing that shirt that is not quite a dress, the one you know is not quite a dress, the one that makes your butt kind of hang out, the only "dress" that was clean. Your boss will look at you at the cupcake-and-coffee meet-and-greet and glare. On occasion, you will be late to work. Sometimes you will be late to work on days when you really need to not be late for work. You will blame it on the subway, or Waze, or your dog. Even if it's true, no one will believe you. You will forget to prepare a presentation on presentation day and have to "wing it," and everyone will know you are "winging it" because your winging is not great. You are a human, and you bleed. You will bleed through your pants. You will finally get the nerve to speak up in a meeting and notice, only later, that you had lipstick all over your teeth. It's fine. Everyone understands. You will not die of embarrassment. You're still here.

Mistakes and unfortunate events like these will happen to you and to almost every weirdo you know. You may even get "in trouble" for them. When you do, don't blow them out of proportion; don't obsess over them. Don't let your weird brain take over and turn this all into the disaster that it is not. The events themselves don't actually matter; how you recover from them does. If something is your fault, don't deny it, don't get defensive, just apologize. Quickly and succinctly. If you can, do it in person: "I am so sorry about today. It won't happen again." Then make sure it doesn't, at least not for a long time. If you're in good standing with your boss, minor blunders here and there are not a big deal. Most managers expect mistakes—they may even secretly love you for your foibles—and they definitely don't expect you to be perfect. You shouldn't expect it of yourself.

Overthinking, Drama, and Other Distracting BS

Most of the things you worry about happening at work will never actually happen—you are not getting fired for that weird e-mail, I am almost 100 percent sure—but there are ways your otherness *can* get in the way of your success. The most basic, garden-variety stuff involves letting your mind go wild and giving too much attention to ghost problems, issues that are not real or that you've created yourself, unnecessarily. I've been working with women almost exclusively for the past ten years—which has been, on balance, a privilege and a delight—and I've been a boss for the past eight, and the number one thing I see negatively impacting talented women is that they get in their own way. They distract themselves with drama or psych themselves out or overexamine situations to a debilitating degree. They fixate on peers at work instead of focusing on themselves and their own projects; they second-guess their in-stincts constantly; they forget to just trust their guts. They per-sonalize the professional, thought-police their managers, and imagine that the people around them are thinking the worst of them at all times.

Here's how this plays out in real life:

"She hasn't answered my e-mail. She obviously hates me."
[Probably she is busy, she sucks at answering e-mails, or she's away.]

"I'm sure she wouldn't want to work with me on this." [You have no concrete evidence or haven't asked.]

"I know how she is." [People surprise you, people change, or you don't know.]

"She never likes anything I do, so why would she like this?" [Gross generalizations get you nowhere. You have nothing to lose, so you should always try.]

"They always give these assignments to Becky—they'll never give them to me." [See above.]

"I'll never get the promotion—X person is so much better than me." [See above. And comparing yourself to others is a silly game, with no winner.]

"That was the worst, right? That thing I did sucked, and everyone knows it." [That thing you did was fine—maybe not perfect, but everyone else was too busy watching kitten videos online to notice. Also, you should never down-talk yourself aloud. It's bad enough that we do it inside our own brains.]

Unless someone tells you directly that they hate an idea, don't want to collaborate with you, or don't like your work, you are better off assuming a positive than a negative. Even when some of what you're sensing is true, the truth doesn't matter as much as your perception of it. Fixating on possible shade, inserting your own narcissism into someone else's bad day, distorting conversations, and projecting negative feelings that don't really exist or, if they do, are slight and insignificant—it's all a slippery slope toward the crazy abyss. Our feelings about work and each other shift constantly. Disasters are temporary; don't get attached to them. Feeling annoyed by another person one day and totally cool with her the next is normal; it happens all the time. You are better off with a default mind-set that you are talented and worthy and smart and have unique ideas, and people want to work with you. Your best work is going to come when you are open, when you can muster enough confidence to think freely and originally. You won't be able to do this if you keep throwing self-sabotage grenades at your own success. There are enough REAL problems at work—sexism, racism, homophobia, classism, transphobia, ableism, egomaniacal bosses, failing companies with little budget to do the things they should. You don't need to damn yourself by creating conflict and making things harder than they need to be.

So take a vow early and often: I am not going to disrupt my own success by getting in my own way. I am not going to let my insecurity monster create a dark, out-to-get-me world; I am going to wrestle it down, again and again. I am going to keep things in perspective, look at the facts, and not allow my negative fantasies to take over my life. I swear to myself that I am going to try to remain chill. I have too much amazing work to do.

The Problem: Being "Fake"

But seriously! I can't do it! I don't know how to be fake! WAAAAHHHH!

You don't have to be fake. Let me repeat: You don't have to be fake. You are allowed to be yourself.

Lest you have the sensation at this point that it's all doom and gloom, you and your weirdness against the masses, I want to tell you a positive story about being weird in a world that is not. The first time I ever went on live TV, I forgot to wear deodorant. I'd been booked to do a segment on spring trends for a local news station, even though, twenty-four hours before this TV appearance, I knew next to nothing about spring trends. (As an editor, I was suddenly qualified as an "expert" to morning show producers; this happens.) It was an early show, recorded live and in the studio; the car and driver they sent (as amazing and fancy as you're imagining) picked me up at 4:30 a.m. Once I arrived, after hair and makeup and while I was prepping for the segment in the greenroom, I started to get nervous. Hives-hot-chest-will-I-pass-out-or-barf nervous. I started to sweat in that way that is true body betrayal, so hard that it showed through my silk blouse. I had armpit puddles.

When the segment producer came to get me, she noticed immediately. Thinking quickly, she summoned two members of the crew to simultaneously blow-dry my armpits before I went on. Because we had less than three minutes of commercial break, this did not occur in a private place, but in front of maybe a half a dozen people—including the host of the show. It was the stuff of your worst naked-in-high-school nightmares.

But somehow in the middle of the armpit-drying session, standing with a group of strangers in full makeup at 6:30 a.m. in a studio in Midtown Manhattan with my arms extended as high as they could go into the air, I looked around, outside myself, and just started laughing. I got out of my own way and was able to see the ridiculousness of the situation. For a moment at least, I stopped taking myself and my life so seriously. Then something strange and wonderful happened: we all started laughing. My sweating incident was bonding. It brought us all closer to each other, and when we went on air, it made the host more kind and generous and silly with me, and the segment was better than it would've been had I not profusely sweated. I was a real, fallible human among other real, fallible humans, and we all connected in the moment.

And this is something I've learned about working that makes me feel better than almost anything else. Sure, you have to be great at your job. You can't just be weird, you also have to be good. And you have to be kind to people. But beyond that, you only need to be yourself. You have to let that freak flag blow around and around at full mast and let the world take you in. It is TOTALLY COOL to be who you are, because this is so much better than trying constantly to be a shiny perfect droid person. You—and everyone around you—will have so much more fun. You will enjoy the experience you worked so hard to live. Say it one more time, with me: You don't have to be fake. Be yourself.

CHAPTER 8

What No One Tells You about Work

S o you got a job, you persisted and resisted, you've survived yourself. *You've survived reading this far into my fucking weird book!* This is cause to celebrate! You're doing it! It's HAPPENING!

So why do you still feel so weird? Let's review:

1. Because you *are* weird and will always be weird no matter what level of conventional success you reach. Most people are.
2. Because offices are bizarro-lands, with oddly shaped furniture and "inspirational" art and humans tossing around corporate jargon as if it's not strange to the ear, as if it's not as awkward as it would be if we all started using 1920s jazz slang as our primary form of communication, or decided to only speak like Vince Vaughn in *Swingers*.

As a society of neurotic overachievers, we spend an inordinate amount of time advising each other on how to ace an interview and conjure the perfect mentor, specifying the precise body language for success and words that we should never put on our résumés lest we be cursed to dead-end-job hell. But we devote little to zero time to supporting one another through the daily discomforts of working, the intricacies and boondoggles and unspoken etiquette and pitfalls that make us feel squirmy and off-balance, the things that we most often obsess and stumble over during our eight- to fourteen-hour days.

Let's Discuss Them Now

1. Your Job, Your Breasts, Yourself

Most career advice is precise. Do this. Don't do this. Do this plus this minus this, keep it a secret and dance around a bonfire, and then you will have job satisfaction, sustained wealth, and internal bliss. But there are few hard-and-fast rules to any of this—only suggestions and best guesses. There is a very real possibility that you could walk into a job interview bra-less, breasts akimbo, wearing a clown costume, and somehow you and your clown costume and your brilliance will win that job because the world is an insane, beautiful place and sometimes brilliant, bouncy-breasted clowns get office jobs. But you cannot count on these unicorn moments. You can't count on sunny 70-degree weather and perfect shoes that look cute and don't make your toes bleed. You can't count on elastic in underwear to stay put. The world is not usually rainbows and ice cream. You need a job, you need to make money, and sometimes that means you have to adhere to some shitty patriarchal office rules. So I am going to temporarily suspend my support for freeing nipples and suggest this about work and your breasts: Wear a bra.

Lest you think this means I am a stodgy pearls-clutcher, I am a big fan of breasts, both mine and all of womankind's. And I am a big fan of liberating those breasts and letting them live their best free life. For a time I had a social tic where I punctuated conversation by flashing my own, which was, if I'm honest, as much about body pride as it was an affectation, a ploy to project a certain freewheelin' fun-girl persona; like how women who want to seem extra feminine scream performatively at the sight of spiders or actively despise the word *moist*. On more than one occasion, I've dashed into work braless, not realizing the shirt I bought from Forever 21 was essentially a dickie made of Saran Wrap, and then, to avoid playing a game of "My eyes are up here," spent the day holding large objects in front of my chest or camouflaging my upper body behind well-placed furniture or plants, the way directors disguise not-written-into-the-script pregnancies on TV. And while we're talking about mamms and work: I've seen 65 percent of my female bosses' breasts, due to circumstances beyond my control. One boss lifted her shirt unexpectedly and said, "Pretty good for a forty-five-year-old, right?"—a statement that was both true and inappropriate.

I'm no boob prude.

And yet.

Here's the truth about your job and your breasts: for most women, without a bra or some kind of underlayer, they're a distraction. That's because we live in a lingering patriarchy where women's bodies are objectified—yes, *obviously*. But it's also because most offices are still all about old-fashioned social norms, and most—no matter how creative—lean on the conservative side. You should wear whatever it is you want to be wearing that is legal in your state to conceal your breasts at work. But you should know that certain sartorial choices are going to be judged differently than others. For example, if you have a work-from-home job and are on a video conference call and you are wearing an old T-shirt without a bra, some people will think you work in your pajamas, whereas if you wear that same T-shirt and a bra, you will look like an upstanding citizen, at least through the Google-live lens. The optics of no-bra-pajamas-plus-working-from-home makes folks assume you are lazy and not taking your job seriously, even if you very much are. If you don't want people to think you are lazy in your professional video chats from home, you should put on a bra. Have a PARTY downstairs—wear nothing, for all I care—but look business up top.

When you're heading into the office, if you don't want people observing your lovely breasts all day instead of observing your professional aptitude, wear a bra. If you don't want people at work discussing your lovely breasts more than they would normally discuss your lovely breasts, wear a bra. If, in meetings, you want people listening to your ideas and not glazing over and wondering about your nipples, wear a bra. Wear a bra to interviews. Wear a bra when the company president comes to town.

Wear a bra because this is the world.

2. Drankin' and Your Job

There was a story, about a hundred years ago now, in the *New York Post* about an office party gone wrong. A young woman, a junior member of a marketing team, got super drunk and had too much fun and then defecated in her pants and passed out. Or passed out and defecated in her pants? In any case, everyone knew she'd done it, everyone knew it had happened. IT WAS IN THE PAPER THE NEXT DAY. WITH PICTURES. It happened on a WHITE LEATHER COUCH. It was a waking nightmare and a cautionary tale, and I still think about it and that poor woman to this day.

Here's a no-duh, The More You Know reminder: if you are an awkward, overthinking person, copious alcohol at a work function is not going to help you socially. It is just going to turn you into a person you are not. And potentially, in your personal apocalypse, it's going to turn you into the woman on the white leather couch.

I say this with years of research behind me. When I lived in New York, I spent ample nights walking into fancy networking parties feeling anxious, making a beeline to the bar, treating it and its accompanying free drinks like my new BFF, and feeling good for a half hour, talking to people I would never have approached without the booze. Then, suddenly, my voice became a wee too loud and excited. I gesticulated a lot too much, stumbled or slurred just the tiniest bit, my even-slight inebriation cracking my confident facade. Ninety-eight times out of a hundred, I spent the next day feeling worried, embarrassed, and like a garbage person, even if I hadn't done anything wrong.

You should drink at the office party if you want to drink at the office party. You should try VERY HARD to not be the drunkest person at the party or the last person at the party, and definitely not both, because then you might spontaneously burst into flames. You should not admit to a person you work with that you *like them like them* at the office party, no matter what *Love Actually* would have you believe. You should not make out with someone publicly at the office party, unless you are completely cool with everyone talking about how you made out with someone at the office party. What you're trying to avoid is letting yourself down, behaving in a way you never would sober. What you're trying to avoid is self-destruction and creating a perception about yourself among your coworkers and managers that is not true to who you really are.

At no time during any drinking work function should you confess your truth to your boss; you should not sidle up to a senior executive someone and spill a company secret, nor pitch an idea you've been burning to pitch. You should not let beer bravery turn you into the employee you always wanted to be at the office party, all booze breath and courage.

One of my bosses secretly despised even mildly drunk people. After witnessing an inebriated employee at a work function, she would regard that person with disdain forever after. This boss was petty and judgmental; she'd bring it up for months, even years. When considering the employee for a big assignment, she would say, "Ugh, but remember how drunk she got at X?" Drinking in front of your boss can color her vision of who you are at work and stop you from moving as far and as fast as you want—no matter how cool your boss may seem.

If you are the kind of healthy social drinker who can trust yourself to avoid all of these things, then by all means DRANK at the office party! But for the rest of us, my advice is: Head to the office holiday party with a full stomach and a plan, a drink maximum and an exit strategy. Identify the important people you want to talk to at the party, talk to them before the alcohol kicks in, say thank you for the party to the other important people. Flirt subtly with your office crush. Then BOUNCE. Jet the fuck out of there with your best work friends and drink all the drinks somewhere else and kick off your shoes and sing some karaoke and gossip about the office holiday party and do you right.

Booze in the actual office is another tricky relationship to navigate. Plastic champagne flutes in the conference room! Coffee-cup servings of chardonnay at Heather's desk! It's a birthday! We won a big account! It's celebratory! Except not really!

Just don't treat the free drinks at work the way you would the free drinks anywhere else. Don't drink them all like there is a shortage of drinks, and by your taking in these drinks, the planet will be saved. Just be cool, take a few sips out of your Dixie cup, and slowly walk away.

3. Sex and the Office

If you asked me, hypothetically, "Is it a good idea to have sex with someone at work?" I would say, unequivocally, no. But life is not about hypotheticals and the moral high ground or always doing the right thing. Life is messy and wild and unexpected and XXX-y and raw, and sometimes there is just someone too good to pass up at work, because he or she is either your soul mate or just an irresistible fuck-mate. If you are going have sex with a coworker, and you care about your job, here are a few *suggested* ground rules.

Try very hard not to have sex with your boss. Because *ew*. Because cliché. Because some evil person will Linda Tripp you, and you will always be known as the person who had sex with your boss.

But. Even. Worse: Don't have sex with your married boss. Or married anyone. Because you respect yourself and other women too much, because extramarital work affairs almost always lead to heartbreak and disaster, because there's not enough in it for you, because it will get out (it *always* gets out) and everyone will titter about it and no one will ever look at you in the same way in that office ever again because the world sometimes sucks. Every promotion you get within that company will be considered tied to the V or D you were catching on the side. You work too hard to throw it all away on a zipless fuck that's fulfilling some creep's midlife crisis. More important, you don't have time for the mess. Screw the boring-hot human you met on Tinder. Have sex with the wan barista in the back of the coffee shop. Do not have sex with a married boss.

If you are sleeping with a healthy, sane someone from work who is not your boss and who is not married, don't have sex with them during actual work hours. Or try not to. Or if you do, don't get caught.

My basic advice on this is to live your best sexy life and be your best sexy self, but don't allow whatever that means for you to get in the way of your career. Make decisions for your future, not for the moment. Because you cannot, in this case, trust the moment. And if you do have sex at work, don't leave any of your underwear on the conference room floor, because . . . just trust me, *because.*

4. Social Media and Your Job: Not Perfect Together

Oh heeyyyyy, I am a person who likes to share all of my feels and things on the Facebooks and the grams and the Twitters and Snaps. And sometimes these things are OUTRAGEOUS and they're snarky and mean because I have the receipts and am getting REAL about lyfe and how I am livin it. Emoji emoji emoji.

Hi, I am a recruiter at your dream job. You sent me your résumé. Your résumé looked great. So I googled you. I just saw your fifteen-pic series titled DRANKS on Instagram and how you shared a story about that dude's penis tattoo on Facebook and hahahah he didn't realize what it would look like when . . . LMFAO! Oof.

Oh wait, you seem dumb on Twitter. Pass.

Oh wait, you seem unhinged on Twitter. Pass.

Oh wait, you have no social media presence at all, and this is a job about marketing and promotion and social media. Pass.

Oh wait, how did you not realize that image/link/sentence/word/symbol/joke is racist/homophobic/awful?

Pass pass pass pass pass.

I know I know I know. We live in a land where personal brand seems paramount. We live in a world where social media platforms can literally make you famous and then literally make you rich. It all feels so natural and instant and candid and alive, and why shouldn't you tell your truth? But most social media stars are not beholden to anyone. They are not representing a company or responsible to a company. Once you sign any kind of full-time, on-staff employment agreement—once you are a category FTE (full-time-employee, in HR speak)—unless you have a clause in a contract that says your tweets are actually your own, you are accountable for what you post. If you post some truly viral-worthy terrible shit, you will make the company look bad, and then you will get fired. Hiring managers look at your social accounts to get a sense of who you are, but also to suss out whether you're a lightning rod who'll be a liability to their business. But even if you're living that freelance life, even if you own your own company and have your own customers or clients, your social media accounts are your calling card. They represent you to the public as well as anything else.

So . . . before you start a job search, give your public social media accounts a scrub. Look at them through a dad's eyes. Look at them through a conservative's and a liberal's eyes. Decide just how well these accounts represent who you are as a business professional in the world.

When you are interviewing for jobs, it's OK—if not recommended—to "friend" or "follow" the people you are interviewing with. But by NO MEANS should you use social media platforms to signal your interest in a position, your impatience with the hiring process, or your eagerness for a start date. You should not "like" or "favorite" or comment on hiring managers' posts to remind them that you exist. They know you exist, and seeing you this way makes them think you have zero chill and are going to be a pain in the ass to work alongside. It could impact their decisions, or make them rethink ones they've already made. No amount of "liking" is going to land you this job. Slow down, breathe, pause before you click.

After you get a job, use social media responsibly. Don't be like that meme of a baboon using a keyboard. Don't pop off when you're drunk or stoned or heartbroken, when you've taken your Ativan and are in between sleep and Ativan madness. Don't subtweet anyone, ever—that is the pettiest shit in the world—and especially DO NOT subtweet your company. It makes you look like an ungrateful kid who doesn't value her job. Save it all for private Snaps. Save it for DMs. Rant all you want to your BFF on WhatsApp. But don't look like a creep on social media unless you want people you hope will respect, employ, and pay you to see you as a creep on social media.

5. How to Write a Work E-Mail and Not Seem Unhinged

Let's get right to it: you are writing bad e-mails. You overthink them or underthink them. You agonize over each word, padding your e-mails with too much information, a sundae of cover-all-bases requests and hedge-your-bets recaps with an overwrought cherry of pleasantries on top. You take too much time crafting the perfect message when the recipient is only going to skim your soliloquy for action verbs, sort out whether they need to respond, and discard it like a flyer for Live Comedy in Times Square. Or you underthink, reacting to each group e-mail upon arrival, rapidly crafting a response, your finger hovering over the reply-all button so you can join the group conversation and get your name on the board, clogging everyone's in-box in the process. First rule of thumb with e-mails: Say less. Second rule of thumb: Chill. Here are the other rules on the other thumbs.

> ➤ Don't write an e-mail when you are feeling angry or anxious or sad or ashamed. Don't speed-read an e-mail that includes critical feedback, get riled up, perhaps misread the message, puff up your chest, respond with something defensive, and subsequently come across as a demented ass. If you are experiencing an extreme level of emotion, write a draft of the e-mail you want to send

and wait at least two hours to send it, after reading it over first. Don't pop off and send something you may later regret. It's in writing forever.

➤ Read your most important e-mails aloud before you hit send. If they sound testy or rude, and you do not want to sound testy or rude, soften the language. Kindness is a choice, and it's an easy one, once you let down your guard and realize that no one can actually hurt you over this e-mail chain. Equally, read your correspondence aloud and listen for overly timid language and excessive apologies. You are allowed to be direct and ask for what you want. Just do it with correct grammar and a few niceties, like "Thanks."

➤ When in doubt, go slightly more formal. (Unless you're writing to someone you know well, and a formal tone would seem spiteful or passive-aggressive.) Use all of the manners you have learned in this world as a civilized human. Be friendly, but polite.

➤ Keep in mind that the person you're writing to is probably receiving dozens of e-mails a day. Be considerate of their time; ask them to do the fewest things possible, and identify the point of your e-mail or what you want help with in the first few sentences.

➤ Consider whether you want this message in writing. Would you rather not have a permanent record of this conversation? Can you achieve what you desire by picking up the phone or walking a few steps to an adjacent cubicle? Would this actually make things less complicated?

➤ Have a goal. Whenever possible, an e-mail should be about one topic and about how the other person can take action on this topic.

➤ Keep it concise, direct, and to the point. Don't include feelings or extraneous information. This is a business e-mail, not a love sonnet or a Dear John letter. You should become the Raymond Carver of e-mail, conveying your message in the most specific and sparest of prose. Before you send, see if there are words, thoughts, or paragraphs you can completely delete and still effectively make yourself heard.

For context, let's apply these rules to an actual e-mail. Imagine you are trying to get paid for something you've written, your payment is late, and you are following up. Here is your first draft of the e-mail.

Hi so and so who has not paid me!

How are you? I hope you are well! I'm so sorry to bother you about this because I know you must be super busy and I hate sounding like a nag. (Please tell me I'm not one of those annoying people who e-mail all the time? This is my worst fear.) Anyhoo: I'm writing today because I wanted to check in about my payment for that story I wrote way back in April. I know we talked about the payment a few weeks ago, and when last we spoke you said I'd have it by June 15th, but now

June 15th has come and gone and I still haven't received a
check.

Maybe it's lost in the mail? My apartment building is weird
right now and it totally *could have* been lost or taken from
the community mail table but I just wanted to see if I should
be worried about this or if the check actually hasn't gone out.

Totally fine either way!

Hope everything is great—I really loved working with you
guys and would love to pitch something else and write for
you again. Let me know when would be a good time to send
pitches or what you guys are looking for.

I mean after this check business is all sorted out. Is there
someone else I can call/bother about this?

Just want to get to the bottom of it.

Thanks so much for your time.

Best,

Person who has not gotten paid.

Here is what you should say:

Hi so and so who has not paid me!

~~How are you? I hope you are well! I'm so sorry to bother
you about this because I know you must be super busy and I
hate sounding like a nag. (Please tell me I'm not one of those
annoying people who e-mail all the time? This is my worst
fear.) Anyhoo: I'm writing today because~~

I wanted to check in about ~~my~~ payment for that story I
wrote ~~way back~~ in April. ~~I know we talked about the payment
a few weeks ago, and~~ When we last spoke you said I'd have it

by June 15th, but ~~now June 15th has come and gone and~~ I still haven't received a check.

~~Maybe it's lost in the mail? My apartment building is weird right now and it totally could have gotten taken in the community mail table but I just wanted to see if I should be worried about this or if the check actually hasn't gone out.~~

~~Fine either way!~~

~~Hope everything is great—I really loved working with you guys and would love to pitch something else and write for you again.~~

~~I mean after this check business is all sorted out.~~

I know you're busy—is there someone else I can call/bother about this?

~~Just want to get to the bottom of it.~~

> Thanks so much for your time.
>
> Person who has not gotten paid.

There is one occasion when you should abandon all of the above e-mail rules. This is when you are intentionally sending a passive-aggressive fuck-you e-mail, a covering-my-ass e-mail, or an I'm-documenting-this-for-posterity e-mail, the contents of which you want a permanent record of with a date and time, basically when you are formally, covertly being a dick for a greater cause. These e-mails are annoying and should not be used frequently, but they're often necessary for recapping live conversations and protecting yourself or your job down the road, or when you are trying to fire someone and are creating a paper trail of how much they suck. You should use these e-mails when an unreliable boss makes you a promise you're afraid she won't keep, a client agrees to something verbally and you want him to acknowledge the terms in a more official way, or you are reporting on problematic events in the office that need to be documented and addressed. Mastering the tone of these e-mails is delicate. You should report the facts while using the least emotional language possible.

If your boss makes outlandish requests, gives you contradictory directions, or flies off the handle about something that is out of your control, you should hang up or walk back to your desk, type up everything he said in a formal fashion, and send him a sunny, clarifying e-mail, explaining, "I just wanted to recap our conversation to make sure I have everything right and can meet your expectations on this project." This way, three months from now, when you are potentially blamed for something that is not your fault, you have the receipts to prove it.

If you have a delusional employee who is spiraling into ruin but thinks she's the best, you should leave your in-person feedback conversations and write down what you discussed. "Hi, employee X, I wanted to recap what we talked about today. . . ."

E-mail can be a smart tool to gain control over an out-of-control situation, to check someone who is behaving childishly or inappropriately or dishonestly, but you must use it judiciously. You don't want to create a hostile work environment if you can avoid it, and you want plausible deniability that you are playing passive-aggressive games, even though of course you are.

6. Muhaha: Your "Private" Work Correspondence Is Not Private

And while we're on the topic of e-mail: You know how your company gives you an e-mail address when you start? I remember this being *very exciting,* and feeling very official when this happened the first couple of times. Jenniferromolini@official-company.com??!! HELL YES. I HAVE MADE IT. I also remember using these e-mail addresses as my primary accounts, too lazy to keep switching back and forth from Gmail or Hotmail or Earthlink or Vonage or whatever it was I had back then. So what I said in my company accounts was everything I felt and everything I did in every part of my life. The messages from my company accounts went to everyone I lived with and partied with and cried with and got naked with; I used them every time I had complained about the company, every time I made fun of the back hair of that person I did not like,* every time I tried to blame not paying my cell phone bill on 9/11 and made a serious, in-writing case about this to AT&T. ALL OF IT.

Then, one day at a magazine where I worked as a fact-checker, Salma Hayek walked in.

I was not a worldly or sophisticated young woman. I did not have the cool veneer that New Yorkers get after being in New York for a long time. Seeing Salma Hayek was, for me, a big, exciting deal. On that day, I rode the elevator with Salma Hayek. Salma Hayek turned to me and complimented my earrings and asked where they were from, and I said "H&M" and she did not know what H&M was and said "H&M, what is this H&M?" and I had to explain and it was *the best.* There was no Twitter, and I had to tell someone this story, so I e-mailed a guy I was seeing, a guy I was sleeping with, a guy I was having a toxic, self-respect-free, masochistic affair with, a guy who also happened to be a reporter. I e-mailed him because I wanted to show off.

---

* Sorry, person. I was a jerk.

I told him because I wanted him to think I was cool. Instead he turned Salma Hayek's office visit into a gossipy story about the place where I worked. He pieced together the Salma Hayek story and a bunch of other details I'd told him about work, and he wrote and published an item online.[*]

He asked me if he could publish the story without using my name and I said yes because I was stupid and because I thought giving him this information made me useful and I wanted to be useful to him. This story made people at the magazine where I worked look dumb. It was embarrassing. It made them *mad*. A few hours later I was sitting in front of the head of HR—a long thread of my e-mails to the reporter printed out in front of me, replete with desperate pleas for him to make the relationship more than it was, awkward attempts to be sexy, all of it from my work e-mail account. This, and the Salma Hayek story.

A half hour after meeting with HR, I was getting my ass handed to me by the publisher of the magazine. This was a man on whom a major *Sex and the City* character had been based, and it was widely understood he was not particularly fuck-with-able. He yelled, he cursed, he reprimanded, he shamed, he outlined the severity of leaking company information, and finally he gave me a break. "You're young and you're junior and I'm imagining you don't know any better, so I'm going to let you keep your job. But if you ever *fucking* do anything like this ever *fucking* again, you're done."

I never did.

---

[*] Looking at this now, I can't actually believe this was an interesting story to *anyone*, let alone to a writer, but the early 'oos were weird.

The company you work for can read your e-mails. They're probably not doing it every day, but they can. They can read your Slack messages (in fact, someone at your company set up all the company Slack channels—that person is the administrator who can play Slack God if they want to). Your company can seize the computer *they gave you* or the phone *they gave you* at any time and find out what you've been searching for and how long you were online shopping and not online working and who you've been chatting and texting and generally talking shit with. Do not type any message from your work computer that you would not want read aloud in front of a room of your coworkers. In front of your boss. Published on a blog, in front of a new employer. Do not say anything that if screen-grabbed by a coworker and shown to your boss would make you lose your job.

7. No One Likes a Note

It seems like the rules of the office kitchen would be simple, similar to those you'd follow in any shared space, the things you learn in kindergarten: Be respectful, ask before you take something, clean as you go, never leave science-project-level food bombs behind. But I've read enough passive-aggressive, long- and short-winded, rude, clever, rhyming, and/or exasperated office-kitchen letters to know that many people with beating hearts still don't inherently understand office kitchen etiquette.

So here they are, simply, though I am sure you are too smart to need them.

DON'T EAT OTHER PEOPLE'S FOOD. DON'T DRINK THEIR ALMOND MILK. WASH YOUR MUG. Remove your food from the fridge before 5:00 p.m. on Friday, or else it will be tossed in the trash and you will have a sad longing for your unopened strawberry kefir.

Oh, and don't leave notes. Notes are never a good idea. Notes make people unhappy, and they make them shame-spiral, and then you have people whose shame leads them to anger and spite, and then ANYTHING CAN HAPPEN. Including a NOTE that answers YOUR NOTE. It's a NOTE OFF! Nobody wants this.

Instead of writing a note, simply chalk up losing half your skim milk to any karma god you believe in. Be smug in the fact that you've paid your debt to society and done your good deed for the day, the week, your lifetime. You gave some needy soul cereal milk. You are a hero. Don't write a note.

8. The Emotional Matrix of Office Bathrooms

The awkwardness of completing one's business in the office lavatory is well-covered territory; it's been fodder for stand-up comedians and personal essayists for years. Once I even saw a major New York newspaper publish a reported piece, a formal exposé *with interviews*, on what happens in the workplace women's room. And what I've gleaned from these reports is that, no matter what the children's classic *Everyone Poops* might suggest, it's still embarrassing for women to poop. I understand. But I don't want to talk about it.

As I see it, office bathrooms are for three things:

Full-length #OOTD selfies

Bodily functions

Tears

These are all private, vulnerability-making events. Be a good human and don't talk to anyone about any of them. What happens in the office bathroom stays in the office bathroom, though I am very sorry to use this tired-ass Vegas slogan to illustrate my point.

9. This Is When You Can Leave the Office

What are the office hours? When can I go home? This is a question that often comes up when I am interviewing new people, and when it does, I wince. I am always nervous that the person before me is about to blow our entire interview by revealing the special circumstance that requires her to leave at 5:00 p.m. every day and letting me in on the special cluelessness that led her to bring this up *right now.* Unless you have an extreme circumstance that would absolutely keep you from working a nine-to-seven day, you should not mention office hours until you know you have the job. You can reject the job over office hours, but it should be yours to reject first. And once you get the job, unless you have a pre-understood arrangement, you should stay at the office until your boss goes home. You should leave seconds after your boss leaves. If your boss is some kind of work/life-imbalance freak who is hiding from his life by staying at work too late with nothing of significance to do, or a person who arrives at 3:00 p.m. and stays until 10:00 p.m. because of what we can only suspect is a rather unrobust social existence or fear of really living at all, you should have a candid conversation with your boss about in-office expectations and see if you can reach an agreement that feels fair.

But, generally, sometimes work will require you to stay long hours. Sometimes you will have to work weekends. Unless you are an hourly employee, you will most likely not get paid extra for this. This is something you will have to suck up and live with. When I worked as a fact-checker, for one week a month I worked until one in the morning. Some of the offices I worked in weren't heated after a certain hour and were also filled with rats who would run by your desk at night. You brought in extra sweaters and learned to keep your feet up. The company paid for a dinner and a car service home. You still arrived by 10:00 a.m. the next day. This was deemed a fair arrangement by all.

Your job doesn't owe you your dream hours. That is the job. If you don't like the job and feel it does not fit your lifestyle, you should look for another job. Do or not do. That is all.

Conversely, staying late at the office for *no discernible reason* just because you think you should, because you think it looks good or means you are working extra hard, or at least makes it *appear* as if you are working extra hard, is an equally wrong-headed strategy. And it can backfire: smart bosses see through hollow, long-office-hours martyrdom. And, trust me, they don't want anyone staying late and getting burned out when they don't have to.

10. It Helps to Strategically Suck

Early in my career, in my assistant days, my boss, Richard, asked me to create a mobile file of all of the phone numbers of everyone in the office so that if he needed to contact people outside of work hours he would have their numbers with him and would not need to track them down. I enthusiastically agreed. I e-mailed everyone with whom we worked and asked them to send me their number. Then I cut and pasted all of the names and numbers into a Word doc, shrunk the numbers to six-point font, printed and cut them out, and glued them carefully onto both sides of an old business card. Then I laminated the card with invisible tape so it would be sturdier. At the end of the day, I handed the card to my boss and told him it would fit perfectly in his wallet. I'd made a wallet-size contact sheet! I was so proud of this accomplishment, of my resourcefulness, that it never occurred to me that he wanted a digital file. I was so proud, in fact, that I don't think he had the heart to explain to me what went wrong.

I have many professional weaknesses. I'm technically challenged, a laughably inferior typist, and a near disaster at most organizational and administrative tasks. When I was an assistant, it wasn't as if I ever felt above the work (a critical distinction; I was always grateful to have a job), I just kind of sucked at a lot of it. What I learned in those early assistant days was that, within reason, it helps to be mediocre at certain detestable parts of your job. If you're valuable and amazing and learn and excel at other parts, the stuff you hate tends to get taken away. This is not to say that you shouldn't try, because, WTF, this is your job, but being bad at menial tasks that are less than thrilling, while remaining overall hardworking, pleasant to be around, and good at other, more critical tasks will lead you to better positions where you do not have to do those menial things. Better still, if you can delegate work to people lower on the totem pole, you will have the best of everything. I have long delegated administrative work to capable interns and then rewarded those interns with coffee or career advice or after-work drinks. It's a fair compromise—they get experience and access, and you get to focus on work that you like and are good at.

One caveat: no matter what it is, and how much you hate it, you should always understand the work you're delegating and be able to take it over in a crunch. However, if you hate inputting data into Excel spreadsheets or filing a boss's expenses, tasks that literally will help you get nowhere ever, you should farm that shit out to anyone you can.

11. But It's Even Better to Be Great

Hidden here at number eleven is one of the most important (and perhaps obvious) things I will tell you in this entire book. You should strive to become, and continue to be, tangibly, objectively great at your job, your many jobs, your career, everything you venture to do. You should channel all of your gorgeous ambition not into of-this-moment professional extensions like your social media following, nor into ephemeral, fleeting concepts like your "brand," but into learning how to do shit, real shit. You should develop concrete skills that can be measured and have meaning, ones you can take with you and build upon over the long haul of your working life. You should learn whatever tangible skills are to be learned in your first job, your next, and the one after that. You should listen to older bosses and learn from their experience, even if you eventually just want to do it your own way. As in any great survivor game, you should make yourself hard to kill—or in this case, hard to fire. If you're a craftswoman, you should dedicate time to perfecting your craft. You should follow the trends in your industry with at least the enthusiasm you'd give to following juicy celebrity gossip or season 2 of your favorite show. You should understand why your company succeeds and how it fails, even if it's boring, even if you hate charts. If you're a creative, you should understand the business side of things, enough so you're empowered and don't feel helpless or lost. Learn how to read a P&L statement. Examine the fine print in your contract before you sign, even if it's making your eyes cross.

Being great means being prepared, putting in more effort than you need to. It means, for an annoying while, being the go-to person, the person who is always more overworked than everyone else. It means dealing with the pitfalls of being the most competent person in the room until eventually you are in charge of the room. Being great means conducting yourself with integrity and honesty and fighting your battles, of course, but fighting fair. This doesn't mean you'll win every job, assignment, or promotion. The world is not always a meritocracy; sometimes it will suck and feel unfair. Sometimes even if you are the most qualified and the best, you'll lose. But competence is calming; knowing you did your best, everything you could, will help you deal with disappointment. It will become a kind of armor, a hedge against self-doubt, a deep well of satisfaction that you can turn to again and again. It's an investment in yourself, a defense against the jerks. It's what you can control. Being great will soften your weirdness; it will earn you patience and accommodation from your bosses and peers. Being great at work, putting in the effort, will help you build a solid, long-lasting career, one with more power and opportunities over time. Even when you think no one is watching, good people, kind people, smart people, the senior people you want to work with and for, recognize this kind of work. *We see you.* We praise your work and talk about how amazing you are in secret boss e-mails we send to each other: "If you ever have a position open, this is the person you should hire." "Oh, I just heard you hired X, that was a VERY SMART move."

We go out of our way for you. We recommend you for jobs you don't even know you want. Your goodness, coupled with hard work and skill, means something, even when you feel most despondent, even when you're dealing with dark office bullshit. Even when you think it does not, your greatness counts.

12. Dark Office Bullshit

Remember how in high school people just didn't like you, for no reason, or for stupid reasons like because you had the wrong-color sneakers or you sat at the wrong table or they just didn't like your face? And these same people maybe bullied you or isolated you or made you feel terrible about yourself or crazy or like you could do nothing good and sometimes even got you in trouble with the teacher even though it was *not your fault?*

This, every insidious, anxiety-producing, outrage-inducing part of it, happens at work too. Sometimes work will seem just like a giant high school, with much of the same bullshit. Sometimes people will hate you because you're new and you're busting up a comfortable ecosystem, one that the current employees have lived within for a long time and don't want to end. Or they'll hate you because hazing the new guy is part of the culture, and it's just what they do. Sometimes it's because you are naturally very good and very efficient at your job, and your goodness and efficiency expose someone else's laziness and apathy and how they've been coasting under the radar, not doing much, for so long. Sometimes it's because a senior person has been over-promoted, and can't competently manage her daily tasks. Deep down, she's insecure, and you, being your competent, best self, make her afraid she'll be found out and lose her job.

Even under the best of circumstances, colleagues are a weird social construct. They're people you're forced to be around for longer periods than anyone else in your life, and because of this many become friends, almost family, by proximity. Just as in high school, you will eventually find the people who are *your people* at work. This will be exhilarating and comforting, but the process should not be rushed. You are not looking for instant friends; you will not find your work wife or husband on the first day. You are looking for true collaborators, real connections to people with whom you will build trust, over time. When you start a job, be friendly to everyone, but focus on observing how people interact, who speaks up when, who gossips about whom, how the boss reacts to it all. Listen, but don't interject your opinions about office life, at least not yet. This may feel lonely for a while, but your loneliness will pay off. Soon the breakdown of the office ecosystem will reveal itself; soon you will identify the slackers versus the workers, the complainers versus the optimists, the scammers versus the generous and kind. Soon you'll know the people you want to get to know more intimately and tell your secrets to, and the ones you definitely do not.

Sitting back now, letting the action happen around you, will put you in a stronger position later on if and when things get weird and dark—when people try to present your ideas as their own, when they cut you out of important meetings or gossip about you in the office kitchen, when they demean you in front of the boss and go for the promotion that should be yours, when your anxiety, social awkwardness, thin or thick boundaries— really, anything about you—earns you the dreaded label of "intimidating."

"Intimidating" is an insult almost exclusively lobbed at women.

You don't hear strong men called intimidating. Strong men are spoken of as commanding, confident; people like how they "tell it like it is," how much they kick ass at their jobs. Strong women, conversely, are seen as a threat, as pariahs; they rub people the wrong way. Unless you are intentionally acting like a dick, being intimidating is rarely about you. More likely it's about other people projecting their feelings of inadequacy onto you. You can be intimidating to other people if you are tall, pretty, noisy, quiet, funny, stoic, shy; if you don't look like everyone else; if you have a unique fashion sense; if you're an intense, competitive person who plays the game of work like Monica Geller plays touch football. No matter how hard you try to bend and appease and please and hide yourself away to make those whom you "intimidate" happy, their feelings about you may never abate.

The best you can do is recognize that "I feel intimidated" is really code for "You threaten me/I need attention and love." Recognizing this doesn't mean you have to transform into a lovable, validation-parroting Furby. If it feels right, you can choose to be more open and emotionally generous at work; if it doesn't, you can simply say "fuck 'em," keep your head down, and focus on your work.

With catty coworkers, don't sweat it too much. It will most likely pass. Just stay above it, hold on to your people tightly, and ride out the storm. Remember that you are not obliged to meet anyone where they are emotionally, especially if where they are is toxic or unhinged. The more visibly upset you get, the more you perpetuate the negativity; the more rattled and distracted you are, the more you give the bullies what they want. Unless the bullying is so extreme that you have objective, tangible proof that it's getting in the way of your capacity to do your job, don't react. Don't rat on the bulliers. Ratting will feel satisfying for the three minutes that you're talking; after that, it will only serve to make the problem worse.

Take the high road. Be considerate and compassionate and empathetic; examine your own behavior constantly. Make sure you are not actually part of the problem, that in your enthusiasm to succeed you are not behaving thoughtlessly or carelessly. Try to right your wrongs, so you can look back at this time and feel good about how you behaved. But don't diminish who you are just to play petty games. Remember that a little kindness goes a long way, but don't cower: just quietly, respectfully, stand your ground.

If it's your boss who hates you, or someone else who has the power to end your job, you may just have to wait it out until you can quit, or get a promotion, or get what you want out of the job. It's the worst, but unless the best decision for you is quitting today (see chapter 10), it's worth it to endure.

13. It's Not in Your Head: Bosses Play Favorites

Just as you enjoy some people better than others, just as your mom probably likes one of her kids the best, and if this kid is not you, you're a wee bit damaged in your core (sorry, moms!), bosses are naturally drawn to some employees over others. These employees' ideas sound better, their requests seem more reasonable, their mistakes and fumbles are more understandable. Overall, favorite employees can do very little wrong. They are just more fun for your boss to be around—and who doesn't like fun? As a boss, when I've had favorites, it's usually people I like and relate to personally, whose work and work ethic I respect and whom I genuinely, inexplicably cannot help but like (usually because they are great; see previous). Sometimes, at some jobs, you will live in the favorite-employee bubble. Enjoy it. Take advantage of it. Take risks. Take your boss's time. Learn. Push yourself and know that you are supported because you are being graded on the "in the bubble" curve.

If you are outside the bubble, know that you're not crazy, and that this is temporary. There's something to be learned from being out in the cold too. Try not to fixate on the state of things; try not to fixate on the favorite person and decide she is your sworn enemy. Do your best to focus on your own experience; do your best to chill. Unless you are a terrible jerk (and even then . . .) the favorite-employee stick gets passed around. You will be the favorite in your next position, with your next manager. You just have to focus and get to your next position with your next manager.

14. It's Not in Your Head: There's a Protected Class

There's a protected class of people in most offices. I'm not talking about people who are formally, legally, often rightfully protected by employment laws—I'm talking about people who suck at their jobs but will probably never get disciplined or fired, no matter how much they fuck up.

This is because they are part of a bizarre "protected class" that exists at companies for a number of reasons. The employee is someone's friend or someone's friend's kid. She is related to someone famous or important. She has information about your boss or the company that your boss or the company does not want leaking out. She's been at the company for a long time, has studied employment laws, and has figured out all the loopholes in the system, and is exploiting them—for example, she is older than forty and has threatened to have a lawyer file for age discrimination, and HR has told your boss to not fire her because the company can't handle the lawsuit right now. Or if she's fired, the company will have to shell out a lot for severance, so it's trying to wait her out. Or if your boss fires her, he will lose head count for this fiscal year, so he'll wait to fire her in January, almost a year away.

All of these scenarios are demoralizing. If you are hustling every day and not in the protected class, it sucks to work next to someone who is not pulling her weight. It's infinitely unfair. But don't dwell on this: identify these people quickly, be cordial to them at all times, and do not let their negativity—or the fact that they exist—drag you down.

15. Money Money Money Money

➤ Sign up for a 401(k). As soon as possible. Have as much money as you can automatically transferred from one money cloud and placed into another money cloud every time you get paid, without even realizing it. This is how you save. Depending on who you are, this might be the only thing that keeps you from living in an abandoned shopping cart in your golden years.

➤ Do not cash in your 401(k). Not to go to Iceland last-minute just this one time, not for your cousin's wedding, not to pay your rent. Not because you think the penalty is not that bad. The penalty is that bad; in fact, it's worse. Also the money you put in today increases at some magic

Rumpelstiltskinian straw-into-gold-thread rate, and if you remove the money from the 401(k), it loses all its magic straw-into-gold properties immediately upon withdrawal.

➤ Always counter on the first salary offer. People will not hate you for asking for more money; they will not think you difficult or rude. They will respect you. When negotiating for a new salary or a rate for your services, imagine the biggest number you can think of, then add 10 percent on top of that because you are definitely still not thinking of a big enough number.

➤ Don't be a flighty-girl cliché and buy outrageously priced "fashionable" items you can't afford just to look fancy at work. These items will most likely not fill the confidence hole in your heart, and definitely not the hunger hole in your stomach when you cannot buy yourself food. That said, don't hold on to your money too tightly—treat yo'self when you can, and enjoy it. Money is what makes aspects of work that suck, suck less.

➤ A sound financial strategy is not to be found in the 1985 Richard Pryor film *Brewster's Millions*. If you spend all the money you have as fast as you can, you will not be rewarded with loads more money. You will simply be broke. This one took me a long time to learn.

CHAPTER 9

The E Word

One day I was on the set of a photo shoot with a pretty brunette actress you know. I was living the goodish life by this point. I had a good job, I lived in a good apartment with an unshared bath, more than one room, and no clowns. I'd stopped paying for the subway in dimes. My on-staff magazine job had loads of enviable perks, and one was that I occasionally interviewed celebrities. Even though the interviews were not long or revealing or deep or serious and were more often focused on trite topics like shopping habits (or, as Avril Lavigne once described our interview, "So this is about accessories and shit?"), getting to do them was a privilege: the assignments were coveted, and it meant the boss trusted you to represent the magazine out in the world. At the very least, it was a chill day out of the office spent waiting for the celebrity in a chic photo studio surrounded by gorgeous people, expensive catering, and the coolest hair and makeup people with the best gossip to talk to all day.*

---

* Hair and makeup people know everything.

On this day, the pretty brunette actress didn't like any of the chosen-for-her clothes, she didn't want people touching her, and she was obviously not interested in any of the stylist's suggestions or advice. This was a problem. The actress had a solution. She walked to the clothing racks, picked out one dress, a giant dress, the most-expensive-of-them-all dress, a red gown. And then she insisted on wearing it backward. You don't have to know a ton about the business of fashion to understand that if a designer lends you their just-off-the-runway gown to be on the cover of a magazine, the designer would prefer that the dress not be on backward, twisted, and lifted up, so it resembles a red fabric tent or the folds of a Shar Pei. But the pretty brunette actress did not care to understand this. Representation was brought over to consult, private conversations in hushed voices were conducted in various corners of the studio, fashion editors went pale, the stylist stomped a foot. They were losing time. *WE NEED TO TURN THE DRESS AROUND.* The pretty brunette actress sat on the floor of the studio, braless, an unzipped, red-dress puddle of protest. She looked up at the crowd of people staring at her, a crew whose day depended on her, at her manager, and the fashion editors imploring her, and said: "This is my being and my person. I need you to respect my being and my person. This is the way I am going to wear this dress." The photographer photographed her in the backward red dress. Another dress was hastily introduced, "just in case," and the pretty brunette actress reluctantly put it on and had her picture taken. The second dress did not look very good. That was the image they used.

Like the pretty brunette actress, we all would like to protect our being and our person against forces that feel invasive, thoughtless, uncomfortable, and even cruel. But like her, too, we need to understand that our feelings aren't always paramount, that we don't always matter more than everyone and everything else, and that sometimes it's actually in our best interest to turn the dress around and STFU because other people need to get shit done. In these situations we might worry that we don't matter at all, and if we don't matter, then maybe the ground will open and swallow us whole. We are often most difficult and entitled when we feel the most vulnerable and insecure.

And this is where perspective comes in—trying to put yourself in other people's shoes so that you can make the best judgment call, so, no matter how intense your feelings, you can put them aside temporarily and work for the greater good. I interviewed celebrities on and off for the next five years. Eventually I grew to hate interviewing celebrities. I understood that the situation was inherently awkward, that the entire economy built around celebrity is gross. I empathized deeply with the subjects, and I liked many of them. But if another pretty brunette actress or blond pop star refused to answer my questions about beauty routines or cried because she hated blue clothes and how could we even think of bringing blue clothes, or because I didn't understand how hard it all was, or walked around naked, refusing to get dressed, or plucked her stray mustache hairs in the mirror when it was time for our interview while pretending I wasn't there—even though she could see me there—or dodged me completely and said that it would have to be a phoner* because she just "couldn't handle" an interview today, I was going to lose faith in humans. Because, ultimately, when you sign up for something, you should try your best to do it. Not to do it is

---

* Gross name for phone interview.

disrespectful to the people around you. Not to do it fucks up people's days. Not to do it says you think you are more important than everyone else. It is entitled, and entitlement is a problem.

I'm loath to bring up the E word here, and I'm even more embarrassed to talk about "millennials" in this way because it is a terrible cliché you've heard a hundred million times, and it is not a cliché I actually believe to be true. However, in writing a book for people in their twenties in 2017, I'd be remiss to not discuss this biggest criticism against them. If you are a twenty-something working in the world of Gen Xers and baby boomers, many older people think you are entitled. This is probably not news to you. Your bosses meet over glasses of wine and get parent drunk and bitch about how lazy you are and how you don't respect authority and don't take initiative and also what a pain in the ass and entitled they feel you are. Boo-hoo.

It doesn't matter that the assessment is a wild, sweeping stereotype, nor that it's not actually true or fair—after managing millennials successfully for years, I know it's not. There's not an entire generation of lazy jerks walking around, waiting to steal jobs and assignments they don't deserve. Also, people of all ages can and do act entitled, and this is just a tidy, cantankerous way to label a whole census block of folks and make them seem less threatening because some people (cough, cough: olds) feel afraid that they might be aging out of their careers and not feel as relevant as before.

Still, when a junior employee arrives on the scene with a know-better attitude—even if it's only a facade that's hiding a well of anxiety and insecurity—along with a list of quality-of-life requests she'd like accommodated, and she brings this agenda to a manager who's been through the job dregs, who was scared to say boo to his boss because said boss would have his ass, the result is a volatile compound of outrage and disdain, confusion and tension. Young employees come in with their many feels and don't seem to hear social cues or know what their boundaries are, and the very best they can expect is that these bosses will become impatient and a little prickly. This doesn't mean your boss is all right and you are all wrong. Their learned behavior is that suffering is just part of the job, yours is that it's not. You need to find a middle ground.

There Is No Entitlement When Humility Is Around

Here is what your boss owes you:

Honesty (but not full disclosure and not full transparency)

Clean, healthy working conditions

On-time pay

Agreed-upon benefits

Equitable treatment; i.e., your boss should not harass you or treat you differently because of your gender, sexual preference, race, or religion.

That's basically it.

Your boss does not have to be nice. Your boss does not have to be fair. Your boss does not have to like you or care about your feelings. Your boss does not have to give you time or mentoring or take an interest in your career or help you meet your professional goals. These are nice-to-haves. You may not be important to your boss; she may have too many people to manage, or, more likely, your issues are simply not that significant in the overall scheme of the company's needs. Your boss may be practicing tough love. She may think harsh feedback and a firm hand are ways to make you strong and good at what you do. She may also be totally selfish and totally incompetent, a terrible person who hates all humans, and puppies too.

Ultimately, this is not your concern. Your job is to identify what it is that you can learn from your current position and then start learning it, sucking this position dry for everything it can give you, meeting the people you need to meet and would like to be on good terms with over the long haul of your career. Your job is to know that you are not the most or even the 107th-most important thing at the place where you work, to handle yourself with humility and treat people with respect, to stay focused and engaged. Your job is to know that you still have a lot to learn, personally and professionally, and that you can learn this just by remaining open, by not interrupting people who have been doing this longer than you. Your job is to wait your turn, and when it's time, and you have a fresh idea, to have the guts to say it respectfully and then listen to feedback thoughtfully. Not to argue or take this feedback personally, not to get in a huff, but to listen and let it sink in. Sometimes these will seem like impossible, Herculean feats, and sometimes you will fail, but in order to live healthfully and productively in your work, you need to try.

Ambition Is Different from Entitlement, and Here's How

I have a theory that the reason so many young women appear entitled at work—why they seem clingy or cocky or clueless or like they're asking for too much too soon and at the wrong time—is that they are afraid to own their ambition and communicate it clearly, out loud. Instead, they skirt around the topic with their managers; they hide behind too-frequent check-ins and fishing expeditions for reinforcement and validation; they ask their bosses to solve their problems and set their career tracks and then grow resentful that they're not getting to do things they want to fast enough, or in their own way.

As women, we are often still afraid to be hungry, to be competitive wolves in the ways that men are culturally sanctioned to be. We cower and hedge and are cagey about our unbridled desire to achieve. We're afraid we can't do it, or that if we can, we won't be liked. Women are taught that our hunger to win is somehow unseemly, unfeminine, or wrong. We're supposed to quietly want it and stealthily get it and not be too public about it in the process. This sets us up for internal conflict and confusion, which leads to convoluted requests and clumsy communication that can be off-putting to busy people in charge. *Ambition is not a dirty word.* When it's pure and real and backed up by hard work, ambition is thrilling, exciting, sexy, and feminine as fuck. But you need to be able to talk about yours coherently, to think about it proactively. Ambition says: I want this—how can I go out and get it? Entitlement says: Gimme.

It's the difference between being active and passive. It's the difference between being a grown-up and a kid.

So how can you be ambitious and not seem entitled?

Be honest. First, with yourself. Identify clearly what it is you want that you're not getting at work.

Make a wish list:

I want to give presentations.
I want to play lead on that account/project/event.
I want to design/write/create _____ on my own.
I want to be in the room and speak directly to clients.
I want to travel for work.
I want to direct.
I want to spearhead new projects.
I want employees who report directly to me.

Examine your place in the organization. Be realistic about your current skills. Instead of dumping your unresolved feelings and not-fully-formed thoughts all over your manager, follow them to where they begin and use them to help you independently come up with a next-steps strategy. Why does XYZ make you feel so strongly or so bad? Why are you so jealous of person X? Why *don't* you pitch your ideas in meetings? What do the successful people have at this organization that you may still be lacking? Do you need specific training? Do you need supplemental education? Did you skip a step along the way, so that X person is always going to be better at X than you are? How can you catch up?

After you've identified the problems, brainstorm ways to solve them on your own.

Take your list and boil it down to immediate action, some

kind of realistic but big-dreams plan. If there are opportunities for you at your current company, approach your boss. At
an appropriate, calm, predetermined time, sit her down and,
bringing with you all the confidence and enthusiasm you can
muster, convey something like this:

> ➤ I love working here.

> ➤ I want to keep working here.

> ➤ I'm worried I may stagnate; or, I'm comfortable with my
>   workload and feel like I could take on more.

> ➤ I've come up with some projects I'd like to start, or help
>   with, OR some skills I'd like to learn that I think could
>   help me stay engaged.

> ➤ Does this sound like the right direction to you?

> ➤ Is there anything you see that I could be working on that
>   could expand my role or stretch my skills, and aligns with
>   your and the company's goals in the process?

Your boss should *love* you for this conversation. You've taken
part of the burden of managing away, and you've shown you're
interested in working hard. Your boss might not have an answer for you about this immediately; your boss may forget to
follow up. If she does, politely remind her about this conversation, about your initiative and awesome, proactive plan, and
ask if you can set regular check-ins to keep your goals on track.

When you feel nervous, remember: You are ambitious, you want things for yourself, that's totally OK. It's great, actually. You are a lovable, competitive, beautiful shark, and you want to keep moving—growing, learning, earning—or else you'll die. Respectfully own this, and you'll be fine.

Good Judgment to the Rescue

Good judgment—a combination of empathy, self-awareness, perspective, and pragmatism—is the thing I look for most in employees. Good judgment involves putting your ego and insecurities aside and seeing the situation for what it is. Good judgment will lead you to respect your boss's time; it will keep you from calling your boss on a Sunday night to discuss an issue that can wait until Monday. Good, mature judgment will tell you not to plan a two-week vacation a month after your last two-week vacation, or e-mail your boss when you're drunk and say you can't come in the next day because you'll be hungover, or have your mom contact your company because you don't think your benefits are fair. Good judgment reminds you to think of other people before yourself, to know that you are special and a unique snowflake, yes, but not any more special than anyone else.

The Not-Entitled Way to Ask for a Raise

Here is the first question to ask yourself before you ask for a raise:

Do I deserve this raise?

Deserve is a loaded word, and it might give you sads and make you feel defensive and like "Of COURSE I deserve a raise. I am the shit." But the answer to whether or not you deserve a raise is not always "obviously," even if your dad strongly believes it is. And this is part of knowing where you stand in your job and the self-awareness you need to bring to your career, because it will help quash all the crazy feelings inside you that happen around work. Understanding the objective reality of the situation, without overthinking and drama, will help soothe your weirdness; it will help you sweat things less; it will make you better at your job. This requires perspective. This requires looking at things through a lens that is not your own. This requires understanding your boss and anticipating what she will say.

Raises happen in all different ways at all different companies, but usually it goes something like this: There is a certain amount of money that your manager can give out at a certain time (usually with an annual review, usually once a year. You can also expect a raise with a promotion, which, if you're moving into a position recently vacated by someone else, can happen almost at any time). A raise often comes from a set pool of money that your boss gets to divvy up that fiscal year. Sometimes who should get the raise is glaringly obvious to a boss. Sometimes it's a little less clear. What you do and how you conduct yourself close to raise time can make all the difference in how that money is divided. I've been thisclose to giving someone a big raise, only to have them pull some seriously irresponsible or dickish or inconvenient-for-me stunts three weeks before I had to make my decision. This meant that instead I gave the raise to someone who wasn't irresponsible, dickish, or making shit inconvenient. Once a boss decides who needs a raise, she submits this information in whatever overcomplicated, blindingly dumb way the company has set up to submit raises (forms, sit-down meetings, dance-offs). Once the qualified person has been identified and this information has been communicated to the person in charge of money, you'd imagine the deserving person would get their raise. Except you'd imagine wrong.

At most companies, raises take longer than you think they should. Raises have to be approved by your boss's boss and sometimes your boss's boss's boss and people in human resources and a finance person too. At many companies, they require an annoying amount of paperwork to "process," with your boss extolling your virtues and why you, and not someone else in the company, deserve this money. I have been in actual conference-call conversations where a group of managers were pitted against each other, each presenting a case for why her people deserved money over the other managers' people. I have been in situations where a raise required the formal testimony of three managers before an employee could be approved. If this sounds insane, it is because it IS insane. It is also a gigantic waste of time, but it's the reality at many big-corporate, big-red-tape jobs.

You should know about these things. You should, in a moment that is not tense or heated, that is not your first month or even your first three months, casually ask your boss what the raise process looks like. If you find out it is a bureaucratic nightmare, you should absolutely still ask for a raise after an appropriate period of stellar work (one year is standard), but you should understand what your boss is in for when she fights to get you this money. And you should not be a pain in the ass when she is trying to do it.

Before I left a recent job, I was trying to get (fully deserved) raises and promotions for a number of women on my staff. The process took months, partly because these things usually take months, and partly because the person handling finances was a disorganized mess with her head up her ass. I checked in every week: "Hey, what's happening with those raises? Are they approved?" And each week she had no answer, or a devil-may-care "I'm looking into it" answer that I could not take action on.

One of my twentysomething employees was impatient and annoyed by this process. She sent me an e-mail asking about her raise EVERY SINGLE DAY. When we had check-ins, she brought it up, every time. Even after I assured her she'd be the first to know, she still hounded me. She would not let it go. She was protecting her being and her person and in the process making me want to kick things into other things. This was not a cool thing to do. This was not keeping shit in perspective. Every time I got one of her e-mails, I wanted to give her a raise less.

Another strategy that raise-seekers employ to speed up the raise/promotion process is the "leverage" technique. This is when an employee puts in the effort to seek out another position, is offered the other position (which she doesn't necessarily want), and then uses this information to threaten her boss: *Hey hey! I have another job now! I will leave if you don't give me what I want.*

I may be in the minority here—there's an argument to be made that it's empowering and upends a rigged system, or at least gets you what you want—but I despise this approach. And as an employee, I've never used it. To my mind, it just wastes a lot of people's time and resources—a great deal of deliberation goes into hiring decisions—and it's not negotiating in good faith. I don't go after jobs unless I truly want them; I don't play games and pretend I'm stoked about a position if I'm not. Equally, as a manager, I don't take the bait in these types of negotiations—usually because I can't, because I've been honest with the raise asker, and if I could have increased her salary, I would have. This kind of maneuver also bursts my comfort bubble, changing my relationship with the employee. I usually see this "fuck you, pay me" strategy as a sign that maybe it's time to cut ties.

All that said, there's nothing wrong with the leverage approach if you're comfortable with it—but be prepared for your boss to call your bluff and not give you what you want, and make sure your backup job is one you could actually live with if she does.

But back to the task at hand: Do you deserve this raise? Here are some easy ways to tell.

➤ Did you not only meet but exceed the goals your boss set out for you, especially in the last six months?

➤ Are you indispensable? Do you do more than your share of work, do things no one else really knows how to do, and/or do things better and faster?

➤ Has there been a change in your role? For instance, you're doing more senior work, you've been given more autonomy, you've subsumed the responsibilities of someone who left recently—there's been *advancement*.

➤ Are you reliable? Have you been reliable for the past six months?

➤ Is there a project you crushed that you can point to in this meeting with your boss?

When you ask for a raise, you are trying to make the case that there's been advancement in your role—that is, something has changed in a positive way to make you even more valuable than before—that you have gone above and beyond in your position, and that you deserve to be compensated for this change, because your value to the company has increased.

These are the reasons you get you a raise. Not just because you want one. Not because you've discovered that the original salary you agreed to is not enough to live on. Not because you found out a person who does the same job makes more money than you do. That's infuriating—but just because another employee negotiated better than you did when they came on does not mean you deserve a raise. You will also not get a raise because another person sucks and you do not. That person will probably get fired, eventually (unless they are part of the "protected class"; see pages 142–43). But that person is not your problem, and if you bring her up to your boss in a conversation about getting a raise, your boss will get annoyed and not want to give you the raise.

Here are some other questions you can ask yourself before requesting a raise:

> When was my last raise? If it was less than a year ago, or you started less than a year ago—barring any big changes in your role—do not ask for a raise.

> Is it raise time on my company's raise calendar? Raises are usually given out at the same time, sometimes once a year, sometimes twice, but usually all at once. You should know when raise time is. Your boss will angle for the

people who seem to need raises the most, the ones who are indefatigable and seem like a potential flight risk. You should be as awesome as you can be at your job, but you should also always appear indefatigable, and therefore a flight risk.

Hey, So Should I Ask for a Promotion at the Same Time?

Promotions are tricky: employees want them regularly, even though their jobs rarely actually change. As with raises, you should ask for a promotion only if you are doing more work than you were before, or you see an opening to do more work than before (someone's left, there's a new project that needs tending, a new employee needs managing), and with a bit of a learning curve, you feel confident you can do it. You should not ask for a promotion if your role has remained exactly the same and you are doing the exact same job and want to keep doing the exact same job. You cannot go from "designer" to "senior designer" just because you like that title better. You have to prove your worth. If you can prove it, ask for it. If the next step up the ladder is not totally clear, research similar positions in your field, have a reasonable title in mind, and present your boss with a plan.

But understand that you do not want to rush your career. This is important: *You do not want to rush your career.* You do not want to be promoted beyond what you know how to do. If you are a twenty-five-year-old "editor in chief" and you really want to stay editing and chiefing for at least the next ten years, but you actually don't know how to edit or chief very well, you are only hurting yourself by gaining an inflated title. Unearned, overinflated titles are worthless penny stocks, and even if it feels very baller now to have this big title, this worthlessness will come back to bite you later on. The more you move up, the more that's expected of you, of course; but also the more you're on display. Big titles mean you get less instruction, less oversight, less mentoring and support. If you don't know how to do your job, you will spend a great deal of time anxious, nervous, frustrated, and compensating for this ignorance with no one to look to for help.

You know how when you take a new yoga or exercise class for the first time, and even though you really want to sit in the back row and hide, you get stuck in the front row and spend the entire class turning around and peering at the more experienced people behind you to see what you're supposed to do? This is kind of what it's like to be overpromoted. You're sweating and awkward and insecure and always looking behind you to catch up.

In an ideal world, promotions or new jobs move you up incrementally, until you're in the front, confident and knowledgeable enough to lead. When you are promoted slowly and organically, when you learn the ins and outs and tricks and become excellent at what you do at each stage, the process leads to balanced, sure-footed success. When you force it, you can fall and break your neck because you didn't know you weren't supposed to twist your head during shoulder stand.

Also consider this: once you reach the top, your ego is likely not going to want to climb back down, and most people hiring don't like to consider a senior person for a less senior role. They'll imagine you are "overqualified," even if you are barely qualified.

Did you actually like this career you entered? Then why rush it? What is your hurry? Why not savor all of the different positions in it; why not have fun, learn all its different facets, make friends, experiment, collaborate, try new things, fuck up, try more new things, get mentored, have less of the boring high-level responsibility and more space and creativity? Once you become a boss, work is more stress and even less fun; you are much more accountable to the big-picture business, to STRATEGY, to serving all kinds of masters.

You should ask for a promotion when you've earned it and when you're ready—when you can do the next job confidently. That's not to say you shouldn't take calculated risks and push yourself out of your comfort zone—you should, and you will—but try to slow down, enjoy the view. Discover your strengths and find your weaknesses and give yourself time to get better and find out what you what you really love doing in this chosen field, the facets of your work that bring you serious, not-immediately-apparent joy. You will never be in this precise position again. You will never have these exact office friends in this exact way. Enjoy yourself. Enjoy your job. Promotion grass is always greener until you find it's just a lonely slab of sod.

Talk to your boss about your career and your goals. Let her know what you want and ask how she thinks you can get there. If your boss says she doesn't think it's time for a promotion, don't get defensive. Be direct; examine what she's saying fairly, and ask when she thinks it is.

CHAPTER 10

How and When to Quit Your Shitty Job

WATCH OUT! This chapter is DIFFERENT! You should not read it like all of the other chapters! Instead you should start at the beginning and read until you come to a CHOICE! Then turn to the page indicated with your choice and see what happens. Each choice will DIRECT and INFLUENCE what happens to you! Each choice will empower you to make the right decision for your life! When you come to the end of this chapter, when you get a new job, you can start ALL OVER AGAIN.

There will come a time when you and your current position should not be together anymore, when it is time to part ways, when you must break up with your job. Like any valuable relationship (especially one that is the sole reason you are able to buy food), it's best to be extremely thoughtful about this decision. Weigh all of your options, stick to your commitment until you've tried everything in your power to make it work for you—see your job to its logical end, and then exit honorably. You do not want to quit until you've gotten everything you need out of your job; you don't want to become one of those pathological quitting people who blames the job for her own inadequacies and unrelated unhappiness. Don't quit until the time is right.

But how will you know the time is right? There may be many reasons you should quit your job, but maybe not *right* away, no matter how chaotic the company is or how unsatisfying the work. Sometimes you need to live with an unpleasant situation as an exercise in personal growth, for the good of your professional reputation, or because you need to pay rent.

Should You Quit Your Job?

Usually when you're thinking about quitting your job, it is not because you are feeling SO RAD AND AWESOME about what you do forty-plus hours a week. Usually when you want to quit your job, it's because you're experiencing some daily discomfort, beyond an acceptable level of daily discomfort. Sometimes this is because your company, job, or boss is hideous, horrible, or abusive, and you need to leave. Sometimes this is because it's a fine job, but you've outgrown it, and you're bored. Sometimes this is because you are expecting too much out of your job—too much fulfillment, too much positive reinforcement or emotional support; you've forgotten that you are there for the job, and not the other way around. Sometimes it's because you are unqualified or a bad fit or you just kind of suck at what you currently do. Before you quit your job, you need to identify which of these situations you're in. You need to go deep and know where you are. You need a strategy and a plan. You need to choose your next adventure.

Follow along, please.

Scenario 1: Your Daily Working Life Is an Anxiety-Producing Shitpit

➤ You are morally opposed to the company's direction. You are made to do things that contradict your code of ethics, like pushing a product you know hurts people; lying about a boss's salacious extracurriculars; giving perfectly competent employees poor performance ratings because you have been forced to implement a draconian HR ranking system.

➤ You are subject to inappropriate treatment—racism, verbal abuse, physical abuse, bullying, extreme overwork without compensation, sexual harassment, insults from your manager, on the phone or over text, off-hours and on—and there is no recourse.

➤ You are asked to do something illegal: cook the books, lie about metrics or financial performance at a public company, give false testimony in any legal capacity, fire a person with a known disability without cause (or, honestly, even with cause).

Is your job this kind of hell? Turn to page 170. If it isn't, keep reading.

Scenario 2: You Haven't "Liked" Your Job in Longer than You Can Remember

➤ You slump into work every day, not just Mondays, not just the day after vacation, wishing you didn't have to be there.

➤ You are ambivalent about every project you are working on.

➤ You spend a lot of time at work Internet-escaping, searching for new fantasy places to live, travel to, get married, Airbnb. Just today you took a quiz on your engagement-ring personality and found out which Jane Austen figure you are, plus you clicked through an entire 105-slide arc of the Rihanna/Drake relationship, only to find the story unsatisfying, inconclusive: Drizzy loves RiRi, but does RiRi love him back? YOU WILL NEVER KNOW.

➤ You have once (thrice? more?) availed yourself of the "mother's room" to take a nap, slipping out unseen, but guilty inside forever.

Do you spend more time at your job surfing for baby elephant memes than you do performing your actual job?

Turn to page 171. If you are miserable at work but in a way we have yet to identify, keep going.

Scenario 3: You Love Your Job, But . . .

➤ There's no room to GROW! You've reached the highest bar in this position, the last ring on the swinging rings course!

➤ You are an eager perfectionist and a serious completionist; you've done all the tasks and tackled all the big projects, and you've been promoted or you tried to be promoted and someone cock-blocked this promotion and you don't know what to do because you love your boss and you love this company but your heart knows! You've reached your ceiling!

If you are a hungry, ambitious bird and need to spread your ambition-bird wings and FLYYYYY, turn to page 181. If not, carry on.

Scenario 4: Work Sucks, Man

➤ You are a person who, if you're honest with yourself and read back over your private DMs, hates every job you've ever been in. You'll get perhaps a three-month runway in a new position when you feel hopeful and semi-engaged, but after this it's all a disappointing slog.

➤ You are a work Eeyore: everything is bad, unless it's worse. But this is just what work is like, right? Work sucks.

Sound familiar? Turn to page 171. If not, keep going.

Scenario 5: There's Something Wrong . . . but Is It Your Job?

➤ You feel incapable of doing the work that is required of you. You're exhausted all the time at work and distracted by daydreams or waking nightmares about other aspects of your life. As much as you sometimes want to, you can't get your head in the game.

➤ You dread e-mails from your manager because you always feel like you're in trouble.

➤ You used to like your position, but recently you barely have the energy to make it into the office, let alone perform.

➤ You constantly feel like you're about to get fired, but you don't know how to make it right. Each time you receive critical feedback, you only feel less capable.

➤ You once enjoyed work, but lately you're spiraling in a vicious cycle of screw-up-reprimand-screw-up and can't seem to break it or catch your breath.

Is your job sucking the life out of you? Or is the culprit something else? Turn to page 174. If you are experiencing normal levels of energy right now, keep reading.

Scenario 6: Work Doesn't Fit into Your Lifestyle

➤ Your job is falling short of your expectations. It's not as cool as you thought it would be, the hours don't allow you to get the sleep you need, party when you want to, or take your *Hamilton* dance class. There's not even a blender for your midday smoothie.

➤ THE ASSIGNMENTS YOU GET? They're INSULTING. EVERYONE ELSE GETS BETTER THINGS TO DO. Ugh, why do these tasks even exist? Why are they *your* responsibility? Why *can't* you spend your day trying to get verified on Twitter? Why can't you expense your $200 sushi lunch? WHY IS WORK SUCH AN UNMITIGATED DRAG?

If you don't understand why your job isn't here for you, turn to page 173.

Your Job Is on Fire

You should quit your job as soon as possible, even if that means going to a lesser job, if you have to. There are certain companies and certain power dynamics that you need to escape in great haste. These are not your everyday "My boss doesn't like me," "I work too hard," "I hate my commute" cry-me-a-river problems; they are not even in the same league as "I'm not challenged," "My boss takes credit for my work," "My voice is not heard," or "Meh, there's no room to grow."

You are experiencing objectively serious, personally damaging scenarios at work that cannot and should not be tolerated. There is nothing compelling enough for you to "stick it out."

If you find yourself in any of these situations, you should quit as soon as you are financially able to quit. You should also consider a lawsuit, but let's not get ahead of ourselves.

If you can quit rightthissecond without a financial apocalypse, turn to page 182.

If you can't, turn to page 177.

You're Bored as Fuck

Here is a trigger moment for you—when you've stopped learning or you are no longer challenged in your job, when you're plodding into the office every day and wishing you did not have to go. If you hate every project you are working on, or your performance is mediocre and you're uninspired and coasting, down on the company and toxic, it's time to start looking for the next opportunity.

Complacency is the death of a fulfilling career. I don't care about your benefits (I mean I do care—I want you to be healthy, but you can find new benefits). I don't care about your vacation days. Phoning it in dulls your senses and your creativity; it's demoralizing to the people around you, it blocks you from achieving your full potential: work that inspires, challenges, and resonates with you comes with more responsibility and ultimately more money and more satisfaction down the road.

You've probably been at your job for a long-ass time. You don't remember what it's like to look for another job or to be in a different company. You've lost perspective on what it is you can do outside this place, in the world. But even if you're not thrilled or even happy, you're *comfortable*. And there's safety in comfort. You know the routines and the personalities, you know the lunch spots, you can do the job while asleep—sometimes you literally are asleep. You've been sitting at your desk for so long you could build a bomb shelter out of the collected swag and office supplies. You are, in many ways, impossible to manage; you no longer give a fuck about doing your actual job, but you give many fucks about keeping your job and getting paid.

Maybe you took this job with high hopes, but have accomplished very little of what you set out to do. Or maybe you've done everything you wanted, and now you're completely stalled. You're rotting in a position because you're too scared to do anything else. If you're going to find work (and probably life) happiness, you need to stop being this person. You need to make a change.

Ask yourself this question: Are you bad at your job? I know, this is a VERY hard question to answer, but it's one you must answer as objectively and honestly as you possibly can before we move on. You must get very clear on this question before starting a job search. If you don't, work will continue to feel unsatisfying or awful, no matter where you are.

Measure yourself against your peers—how is your work performance compared to theirs? Look up a job description for the job you do and think: Have I mastered all of the skills in this position? Do I excel at this work? Do I want to excel at this work? Do I like what I do—not in this job, but at this company or in this career? If not, what is it that I actually want to do?

Before you continue down the "This job sucks, fuck this, I hate it. I want to do other work that doesn't suck" road, you need to understand the core problem. Know thy work self; it will set you free.

Would you like to continue what you're doing at the level you're doing it? Turn to page 177.

Do you want to try something completely, outrageously different? Turn to page 175.

You Hate Working

Not to be confused with being bored AF, because bored people actually like work when they're challenged and engaged. You are more the . . . chillax-and-get-paid type. You would like to do the minimal amount of work possible and spend the minimal amount of time at the office possible and still get your paycheck every week. You are the type of person who comes in late with no apologies, blows off assignments and meetings, and afterward tells your boss that you really need to get your hair highlighted this afternoon, it's the only time the stylist can fit you in. You have a filibuster-long list of needs you would like your boss to meet, but you rarely think of the needs of the business. You are not motivated by traditional success, or by money, or by doing the right thing and not pissing people off. Somehow you missed the lesson that, to be productive members of this human world, we need to work. No one has helped you understand accountability. You think your way is right when your way is obviously not right. When working, you give very few fucks about changing your behavior so you don't get fired, but when you do get fired— and you get fired a lot—you are shocked and even outraged. You write nasty posts about it on your blog. You tweet about it. You gram your sads and mads. The injustice! I hate to be the one to tell you this, but you are a boss's worst nightmare.

Turn to page 179.

It's Not Them, It's You :(

You are lost in this job. At this moment, you may be too hurt inside to work. There is no objective measure of pain; you might be going through a heart-wrenching breakup, something in your life may have triggered an early trauma, your dog may have died, you may be seriously depressed.

Here is a hard truth: it is not work's responsibility to know when you need to bow out, either temporarily or for a while. You are in charge of your own self-care. When you are burned out, when you are emotionally drained, when you just *cannot* anymore, you need to get really deep with yourself, identify the resources available to you—time away in the short term, mental health support in the long—and get control. You do not want to lose a job you love. You do not want to get fired and burn a bridge. Most important, you don't want to let yourself down. Take care of yourself. No one else will. Get honest. Get help. Any boss worth his salt will support a good employee during a difficult time, but you need to sound the alarm and present a viable plan.

After taking a self-care break, if you realize that you can no longer do the work you signed on to do and you want to make a change, turn to page 175.

If you want to keep doing the same work, just somewhere else, turn to page 177.

Big Ch-Ch-Ch-Changes

You need a change. You don't want to do what you do anymore. You want to try out a career as a stand-up comedian or a social worker or a teacher or a mime. Maybe you still enjoy your field but are not satisfied by your specific area of work. Maybe you've moved far down a path into a position you hate, and you need to back up to that fork you passed and take the other road, the road that's less management and more creative, less pressure and more fun.

Creating the big shakeups in your career, the ones that bust you out of complacency and into action, requires taking calculated risks, betting on yourself and betting that you'll win. Once you've recognized that you've gone as far as you can in this particular position, once you've acknowledged that the drudgery of punching the clock is not a viable option for you in this one beautiful life, you will have to hustle anew. This hustle will require a period of sacrifice—inconvenience or lost sleep or lost money or lost Netflix sessions or lack of your fave time spent sitting on your arse. The good news is that you've identified your own unhappiness and dissatisfaction: the time to begin taking your risk is now. You are not going to get less scared. Just like when you were first starting out, let your new dream slap you in the face. Identify what it is you want to do, and sort out what experience or training you'll need to do it. Unless you can responsibly afford to say "Fuck this noise" and mic-drop your job, you should use your current position as a holding cell for as long as you can, a way to pay your way in the world while you pursue your new goals on the sly. Can you work during the day and attend classes at night? Are there skills you can learn at this job that will help you with your new career? Does your company have tuition reimbursement or support? Is it possible to change your role temporarily, take a leave of absence, or have a more flexible work-from-home schedule?

Changing your life is exhausting; there is no quick fix. But once you've completed the transition, once you've gained the training or experience you need and feel safe enough to leap into something new, or you can confidently afford to quit and just begin down the path to something new without the safety net of your current paycheck, you can quit what you're doing now. Hurray! Hurrah!

Turn to page 182 to find out how.

Not Dumb—Lateral Moves

In the best-case dream scenario, every job change you make in the same career will lead you to a better and more senior title, more responsibilities, and buckets more cash. But if your job is on fire, or you love your exact role, but not in this exact place, or you don't feel aligned with your current company and its current work culture or goals, there's no shame in making a lateral move—especially if it suits your current needs. You should make a lateral move if you need to get out of a job fast and it is the best option presented to you. You should make a lateral move if you are looking to go in a different direction in your field—if you're trying to update your skills and stay relevant and need the experience of a different, more modern, cooler kind of company to make yourself more professionally viable, long-term.

This could mean moving from a small firm where you are top cheese to a big firm with more prestige where you will be a smaller, more chill fish. Or the opposite: you are but a minnow at the ginormous organization you work for now, and you'll accept the same title and salary at a place where it actually means real influence. This could mean jumping from a stodgy, out-of-touch company to something younger, slicker, hotter, with more cultural currency. It might mean taking your universal skill set (money things, human resources, computer systems) from a business that you no longer believe in to one you love and feel passionate about. There are so many aspects to consider—location, lifestyle, benefits, perks, where you want to go next. In some ways, your right-this-minute job search is about looking into a crystal ball to two jobs from now: What should you pursue now that can lead you to what you want next? In five years? In ten? Modern-day industries change far too fast for employees to think about until-retirement forever— some of the positions I've recruited and have been courted for* didn't even exist that long ago—but having a firm grasp of your goals for the next two positions will help you make smart, informed decisions about what to do and where to go next.

Once you've landed your rad new lateral-move role, turn to page 182.

---

* Editor in chief, Red Bull.

Your New Planet

"WELCOME. YOU'VE ARRIVED!" says your new planet's greeter, who looks like that boy you bullied at your first job at the fourth-grade car wash, with a twinge of the store owner you stole from in high school. "WE ARE GLAD YOU MADE IT. YOU WILL STAY HERE FOREVER NOW. YOU WILL NEVER LEAVE."

"Why?"

"BECAUSE NO ONE ON EARTH WANTS TO WORK WITH YOU," says the Boss Queen, who looks like the intern you made cry that one time, coupled with the colleague you once called "Chubs."

"I will try harder," you say, but you don't mean it. You hate trying.

"NO. YOU ARE STAYING WITH US," they all say in unison, the army that's emerged with the faces of every boss you've ever flaked on or fucked over, every former coworker to whom your carelessness caused pain.

"FROM NOW ON YOU WILL GET COFFEE ALL DAY FOR WHOEVER WANTS IT HOWEVER THEY WANT IT AT THE WORLD'S MOST INCONVENIENT STARBUCKS, THE ONE THAT'S EIGHTEEN BLOCKS AWAY. YOU WILL TRANSCRIBE INTERVIEWS. YOU WILL ENTER DATA. YOU WILL FILE THINGS INTO OTHER THINGS. YOU WILL PREPARE 159 POWERPOINTS AND 23 EXCEL SPREADSHEETS PER DAY. YOU WILL MODERATE COMMENTS SECTIONS ON BREITBART. YOU WILL BE ON AN ENDLESS LOOP OF CONFERENCE CALLS INTO ETERNITY."

You try to check your phone, to Google an escape. You switch over to Snapchat to tell this story live. You attempt to text your bestie a scared-face emoji. But then you realize: the Wi-Fi signal is too weak. There's only one way out: you have to put in the time, be kind to the creatures, stop complaining, care about and become good at working. Then, and only then, will you be released.

If you feel you can learn to responsibly work somewhere, just not at your current job, turn to page 182.

The Big Step Up

You are ready for a new challenge in a new place in the same field. You are a hypersuccessful, determined, talented, hard-working employee, and you want to move on to a higher-level position with more responsibilities, more money, and a bigger title. You have been where you are now for a while; you've learned everything you could or should, and you are ready to bounce. You have visualized the next rung on the ladder, and you are ready to go for it, as fearlessly as you can. You may have already been recruited for something new, something exciting and engaging and cool. You've updated your résumé and brushed up on your interview skills. You bought a new outfit you're excited to wear. You got this.

If you haven't been recruited, it's time to start looking. Start kicking the professional tires, talking to everyone you know and trust in the business. Let them know—quietly, discreetly—that you are thinking of leaving. Identify the companies you most want to work for and reach out to any connections you have there, just to check in. In the meantime, get all the extra training you can in your current job. Manage all the employees. Take on a high-profile project that you're sure will succeed. Keep a record of your best strategies, ideas, and wins. Attend more networking events in your position. Talk to headhunters and tell them what you want. You're on the market. Get yourself out into the world. You're a dream employee. You'll be scooped up soon.

Once you are, flip to the next page.

Here's how you quit your job.

OK! So you have the next thing all lined up, and you feel happy and secure, or at least relieved and excited and terrified. You've signed the papers on your new thing, you've given the new place a start date, you've got an actual offer in your hand or on your e-mail, and it is unequivocal that you indeed have a new job. OR, if you don't have another job, you have made a realistic plan to pay for your housing and your eating after you end this current gig.

Only now, at this precise moment, is it OK to give your notice, or to tell anyone that you were looking for a job or thinking about leaving this one or that you've found a new opportunity. The way you leave speaks volumes about who you are and how you will be remembered—whether you will ever get a good reference from these people at this place where you spent all this time, or if you will burn a bridge and be resented forever. This is a moment that can come back to bite you. This is also a moment when you can truly step up to rise above creeps and haters, the tormenters who have made your life hell for all these months or years. They might not deserve your respectful exit, but you owe it to yourself to keep it clean, to be the amazing professional you are and will be.

Here is the protocol for quitting:

You should tell your direct manager first—in person, if at all possible, and if circumstances don't permit this (i.e., you live in different cities, or she's always away), over the phone.

You are not obliged to give your manager the real reason you are quitting—at this point it will just seem petty and like sour grapes anyway. Save your constructive griping for the anonymous "exit interview" with HR, which is probably not anonymous, but who cares. You are also not obliged to tell your old boss where you're going. You can keep your future plans a secret. The only thing you still owe is to give proper notice and work out the last days of your employment respectfully, and not to burn the place down.

Keep in mind that, once you give notice, you give away all of your power at your current job. Your resignation signals the HR machine to start running: you have lost all agency, and your bosses can walk you out of the building within minutes or hours if they decide to. They can say, "Hey, great, sorry to see you go, give me your computer right now." They can say, "Actually we'd like you to leave today." If you have clients—or writers or accounts, or anything that you oversaw under the company umbrella that is critical to their livelihood—they will immediately try to take them away from you and wherever you are going. If you have ever seen *Jerry Maguire*, it's like that, except less dramatic and without the fish.

Up until the moment that you give your notice, you carry all the power. You have a secret. You should capitalize on this by preparing for every worst-case scenario—wiping your computer clean of personal files, downloading your contact lists, taking home your office valuables—imagining they could kick you out of the office forever the moment you resign. You should not *absolutely need* the money coming in from your two weeks' notice for something as desperate as rent or food, because the company might not let you work those two weeks. You should be prepared to walk out the moment you give your notice. These scenarios will most likely not happen. But you should be ready for them if they do.

Unless you are on amazing terms with your bosses AND finishing up a big project, you should give two weeks' notice. You should not give more because you feel bad, because you think it's the "right" thing to do. Do not give three months' notice, thinking this makes you a generous, thoughtful person and everyone will love you and be grateful to you for this self-less, angelic gift. Too much notice is a gift to no one. It traps everyone in the past. What happens when you give too much notice is that, much like the image of Marty's family in *Back to the Future*, you slowly start to disappear. You will become a walking-around-the-office ghost. Your opinions no longer matter. Your bosses and colleagues will start having meetings without you, and this will make you feel weird and left out. Important projects, projects that you loved and felt protective of, will move on in new directions that you do not like and are powerless to change. Hiring and firing decisions will be made without your approval.

No one knows how to behave in this awkward notice-period purgatory. No one knows who should make decisions; there are no socially sanctioned rules. If you extend it, it only exac-erbates this confusion and makes the situation worse. After giving too much notice once, I arrived at the office weeks be-fore my last day, only to discover my personal effects—years of confidential and personal files, tokens and office memo-ries, private correspondence—dumped in a public corner like junk on the street, like those homeless-people sidewalk sales that sell used candles and one of a pair of old shoes. Apparently the afternoon before, while I was out, another manager who coveted my desk decided it was a good time to move in and cleaned it out. No one notified me. No one stopped her. No one cared. We were living in too-much-notice purgatory, and it was clearly time for me to go. I packed up the contents of my homeless-person stoop sale. I had a drink at the nearest bar at 10:30 a.m. I never returned.

Don't be overly considerate in a world that can be thoughtless and crazy-inconsiderate. Think of yourself first. Give two weeks' notice.

CHAPTER 11

Fashion Magazines When You're Not "Fashion-y"*

A fter two years working as the Chill Out editor, I come to be hired at a fashion magazine. I say "come to be" because I don't go after this job; it lilts toward me and finds me one afternoon when I am sitting at my desk, late on deadline, deep into a vending-machine snack coma, Fritos dust dotting my cheeks. I receive a call from the assistant to the editor in chief of the fashion magazine. The editor in chief wants to see me. She's seen my stuff. She likes it. The call is coming from inside the celebrated building that houses the famous media company with all of the *best* magazines, the one that everyone talks about, the one that's in the movies. It's

---

* This chapter could have easily been titled "How to Survive the Job You Have" or "When Life Gives You Lemons" or "Square Peg, Round Hole." But I liked this title better. Suffice it to say, it's about making the most of a seemingly bad situation and how there's value in every position you'll have.

a call you can't *not* answer. It's a call people would give a small toe to get.

Still, I am reluctant to go to this fashion magazine. I am leaving a job where I get company-sanctioned facials during office hours, where I get to write about people who make acid-trip art, where I smoke pot with Woody Harrelson, where my literal title is *Chill Out editor.* The people at my current job are *my* people—salty and weird and wonderful. Some of them wear Christmas slippers to work. This job pays me approximately $3 a year. When the big, rich fashion magazine calls and the editor in chief offers me a grown-up salary, one that's more than double what I am making, I go because I haven't paid my phone bill on time for approximately forty-seven months, and because I am not stupid.*

When I arrive, the office smells like perfume and frosting. It's my first day, and the editor I am to report to is planning her wedding. She can't decide on the Louboutins or the some other designer name I don't know. Everything looks too *creamy.* She is fatigued by this process, *you have no idea.* The cafeteria is downstairs, just a few floors below us. It has a stir-fry station, though no one eats the rice, and a sandwich station, though no one eats bread, and garlic-free hummus and garlic-free Caesar salad dressing. There is no garlic allowed anywhere in the cafeteria, someone explains; there are only certain times you should go. Our office is located on the lower-level elevator bank. Other magazines are on the higher-level elevator bank. It makes a difference. You're allowed to expense cab rides, the magazines you buy at the downstairs kiosk, lunch, sometimes

---

* Well, not totally stupid.

drinks, but not too many and not too often. There's a "free" table filled with castaways from the editors' free stash; off-brand body scrubs, velvet socks, books on gardening, sporks. (Some people check the free table many times a day; you shouldn't be one of those people.) The company awards its most valuable employees with private cars and private drivers. The cars are all the same, black and boxy. At pickup time, they clog the Midtown Manhattan street below like too many ants marching toward a single crumb of cake.

The office is organized into multiple departments—fashion, beauty, art, copy—but it's really sorted by Chanel-haves and Chanel-have-nots. There's *stuff* everywhere—desks and nooks piled high, closets overflowing, the hallway to the bathroom lined with racks upon racks of clothes. It's a hoarder's frenzy of acquisition, a reminder everywhere you look of the caste system of the place, who gets to pick, touch, play with, and often *keep* the stuff, and who does not. The mail comes once a day, bulky packages and soft envelopes, giant boxes wheeled in from some space in the building I never see. Messengers arrive hourly, toting game-show-prize-level loot straight to corner offices and adjacent cubicles. It's Christmas every day. Assistants keep box cutters in their pen cups as if it's a requirement of the job.

Fashion editors get reams of clothes and sometimes jewels, but beauty editors unexpectedly pull the best haul: Marc Jacobs wallets, Gucci totes, elaborate cakes and magnums of champagne to wash them down, all-expenses-paid sojourns to the South of France and front-row concert seats, $100 candles, luxury-line cosmetics, lotions and parfums and parfumed lotions. They carry out the spoils each night in oversize shopping bags with ropey handles, on their way to events where they will score more stuff.

For the first few months, I don't really understand my job. I've been hired as "staff editor" to edit and write, but there's no sense of order or scope, what I am actually accountable for and what I'm not. When I try to get clarity, I'm told I'm not a beauty person and I'm not a fashion person, I'm a "utility person."* One night an editor invites me to her apartment for drinks. When I arrive, before I go in, she says, "Now, don't have class issues."

The office is a powder keg of hazing and agreement. There's a groupthink mentality among the higher-ups, an entitlement to get and be given: they want the free clothes *and* the six-figure salary, they want to fly first-class on business trips *and* pilfer coffee from the office kitchen to bring home to their nannies. They want a better downtown loft than the one they have, they want the one that was featured in the Homes issue of *New York* magazine, the one that belongs to the woman whose husband is in mutual funds and not in investment banking. They want to be profiled in magazines. And sometimes they are.

Meetings begin with outfit assessments, examinations up and down: "Cute. Cute. Cuuuuute. Cute." Or: "You can't pull off that bubble skirt. I don't know why you thought you could." One day a senior editor decides to give everyone a "Patty P" nickname and goes around the office pointing and calling out, "Patty Perfect!" "Patty Pretty!" and, when she gets to me, "Patty Portly." Another day, when I attempt a perhaps ill-advised braided hairstyle, I'm

---

* Years later I discover this is a baseball reference, one that, like any sports reference, sails miles over my head.

told, "It's hard to make a pretty girl ugly, but somehow you've managed." I cry nearly every night after work for weeks.

Everyone is not awful and everyone is not like this; most of the people working there aren't. I make my own community of friends, a cadre of smart misfits and outliers with whom I will form deep, close friendships, whom I will know for years. The boss, the reason I came (besides the livable wage), is brilliant and complicated, straightforward and intense, detached from (though still in some way complicit in) the coven. I'd followed her career for more than a decade before I got the call. She is an editor-hero. For a while she is the only thing that makes me feel normal, OK, and like I can do the job. I do not see her enough, but when I do, I *learn*.

Editing is subjective, editing is precise. Editors often lack vision and are often full of shit. Editors hide their lack of talent behind arbitrary changes, behind flimsy direction and nebulous phrases like "punch it up." But the editor in chief of the fashion magazine is not this way. She is tough and exacting. She gives clear, concise instruction. She red-lines everything I do and makes me do it again. And then a third time. Keep doing it until you get it right. She has a nearly hundred-word "banned word" list that no one dare use. It includes cloying phrases like "to boot," "run, don't walk," and "rock star," and detestable adjectives like "yummy." She allows us to get creative, to add *y*'s onto words like *fashion*, but she is not keen on it. She is right 99 percent of the time; sentences always sound better after she touches them. She is as obsessed with and obsessive about the work as I am. She teaches me that there are no dumb topics, only dumb descriptions; that in the right hands, even a frivolous caption about a dull pair of jeans can be elevated to affecting slant-rhyme, a skill I use—and teach—to this day. I will learn more from her about writing, editing, voice, audience, and my own talent and skill than I will from anyone else in my career.

I begin the job—and remain to this day—desperate to impress her. The first time we are alone in her chic, all-white office, I am so nervous that the corners of my mouth twitch, and it is difficult to form words. I laugh too loud, a spitty chortle, really. I agree too much. I am afraid I am annoying all of the time. I probably am.

There's a uniquely intimate dynamic that happens between some female bosses and female employees, a tendency, at least early in your career, to idolize the person in charge and/or turn her into a mother surrogate, to make her approval paralyzingly important, critical to your survival. If you let this dynamic go too far, if you build up your boss as an infallible, bigger-than-life presence and tear yourself down as a lowly turd human, you will erode your confidence and distract yourself from learning and doing great work.

To strike a balance between ohmygod-I-love-you hero worship and self-respecting levels of deference to a boss, you need to recognize that just because a person knows more than you, that does not mean she is *better* than you; she's just been doing it longer. You can respect someone and hold her opinion in high regard and still respect yourself in the process. You must remember that you have value as exactly who you are, exactly in this moment. This will take practice.

Over time, I learn that the editor in chief is, in fact, a flesh-and-blood woman and not just a hologram of all my professional aspirations and repressed mom issues. Over time, she confides in me. I find her acutely human. We hang out outside of work, but then she reminds me of the job, of something I did wrong; I remember the power she wields over me, and I feel afraid. We are friends, but we cannot be friends. I learn that the next job cannot be like this. After I work for the editor in chief, I learn to have "boundaries" with bosses. It is necessary. It is also a little sad.

After months on the job at the fashion magazine, I finally begin to assert myself. I slowly carve out an identity and a space that is solely mine. I ferret out precisely what it is that I bring to this strange table. It's true that I am not a fashion person and I am not a beauty person. I am in fact a utility person, and there are not many of us around. I move stories along quickly. I edit pages upon pages each day: *pass pass pass pass.* I am a fast-moving and efficient part of the assembly line. I feel proud.

I begin to join group e-mail chains and speak up in meetings. Initially, everything I say is wrong. I don't know what chevron stripes are, I don't know Goyard. I say "gorgeous" when I should say "glamorous." I call something "luxury," and it is clear that I have no idea what luxury actually means. I offer up story ideas, and they are politely ignored or given the same "ha ha great" enthusiasm you'd give to a plate of steamed beets. But eventually the percentages shift. Eventually I am able to anticipate the boss's needs, to replicate the editorial voice, even to teach other people how to do it. I buy a fashion dictionary and the world's thickest thesaurus. In my free time, I read fashion biographies and I study fashion magazines. I am fixated on cracking the code. I become very good at my job.

It is a job that feels "not like me" and "not for me," but I find that this is immaterial, that excelling at it brings a level of satisfaction I did not expect.

For three years I am given work that no one else wants, sections that are considered unsavory by other editors, areas that the women who pronounce *luxe* "loooooooooxs" have no desire to touch. I turn this into a positive. Print editors *hate* dealing with the website—they print out the web stories on paper, mark them up with colorful pens, and hand them over to web editors to input changes online, even though this is a maddeningly inefficient way to work, the equivalent of that bad joke about blondes putting Wite-Out on a screen. I help edit the website, I befriend the web people. I learn the technology. I write a blog. I accumulate an entire new set of skills, skills more relevant and important than I even know—skills that will get me my next job and propel me into an entirely different part of my career.

Because I am nervous that I will be pigeonholed as a "fashion" person and limit the scope of my career, I continue to write on the side, about topics I care about, for publications I admire. I work most weekends, and after eleven attempts to pitch the same story, I finally see my byline in the *New York Times*.

In my last year and a half at the fashion magazine, I make a wish list of everything I want to achieve before I leave. (Allow me to reiterate: make wish lists.)

1. Manage someone, anyone really
2. Write cover stories
3. Have a regular, in-print byline
4. Write daily for the website
5. Make more $$
6. Get a better title

I do not include "Address the persistent chip on your shoulder" or "Stop acting like an angry asshole"; I leave those to-do items for some future me, down the line. I consult the list every month to track my progress. I negotiate it slowly and awkwardly, over time. Into year four, I am named deputy editor of the fashion magazine, checking off the last goal. Three months later, I quit.

My next job is as an editor at a big tech company. The dream has changed. I will never work in magazines again.

CHAPTER 12

What I Wish I Knew

O ver the decade or so since I officially became an editor, I've sat on a number of conference panels, with a number of silly-formal conference-panel names. I've given speeches with post-speech Q&As, been a guest speaker in classrooms, and been interviewed about my career for publications, both biggish and small. The questions I am asked in these situations range in quality and scope—sometimes people want to know old magazine yarns, sometimes they want to talk about *womyn* on the *Internet*, sometimes about something real sexy, like how brands can reach an audience across platforms. But most of the questions I get involve advice—*What's your advice for young editors? What would you tell new college grads?*, and then, if the moderator/interviewer/question-asker is trying to mix things up, *What career advice would you have given yourself?*

This question is an old trope, a popular magazine-essay packaging device, a way to make an audience simultaneously sentimental about wisdom and nostalgic for youth. We see variations of this self-advice construct in web articles, bundled up in "Letters to Myself" books, in videos where semifamous people fade into one another as they espouse inspiring aphorisms about life. It's intimate. It's navel-gazing. It's nurturing. It somehow flatters us all.

Whenever I am asked this question in public, I don't really know what to say.* The real advice I wish I could give my younger self is more intense and harsh than what I'd give to others, what I'd give to you. It's not a sound bite, it's not onstage cool. What would have been most useful to me in the early stages of my career, during the period between first-job terror and middle-management malaise—in addition to all the more general advice you've read so far in this book—is embarrassing and intimate. It's tough love. It's not always nice. Here's what I would have told myself. Maybe it will help you too.

You'll Suck at Everything the First Time You Do It

You will probably suck the second and third time too. Don't get defensive about this; don't decide that you should never do the thing again because you're as worthless as a chin zit. Don't compare yourself to other people who have been doing the thing longer, who have practiced and are better. Who were maybe born better—who cares. Don't pretend the reasonable person critiquing your work is wrong and awful and your sub-

---

* So I say something canned, like "A little sugar goes a long way!" Or something I think will get a laugh, like "Wear a bra!" Hardy har.

standard work is up to snuff because believing this soothes your ego. That thing you did sucks, but it doesn't matter: with effort, you can become great at almost anything except maybe (at this point) professional sports. Accept this as reality, stop getting so mad, stop being so mean to yourself, and start working to make it good.

There Will Never Be a Positive Consensus about You

Some people just won't like you, whatever. There's no amount of extra-teeth smiling or forced charm or jokes or compliments or social games or happy-face emoji DMs that will change their minds. Sometimes people just won't like the cut of your jib. Sometimes you will say or do the wrong thing, put your foot in your mouth, and cause irreparable harm. You're human, you fuck up. Don't fixate on this. Don't clap back. Learn from the situation and move on.

Stop Vacillating between "I Am Garbage" and "I Am God"

This is annoying. And it's exhausting. All these self-esteem swings are tuckering you out. You don't need to be one or the other. You're in the middle. Everyone is. Even Kanye. Moderate your ego. Do your best. Seek out new opportunities. Don't be afraid to take risks. Some days you will feel good about your work, some days you will feel bad, but all days you are fundamentally the same. Ground yourself so you don't crave constant validation, so that every accomplishment or positive reinforcement, every negative comment or rejection, doesn't redefine who you are. Call your grandma. Do something kind. Think about someone else for a while. That will help.

Chill the Fuck Out

You're taking work too personally and too seriously, you're confronting people too much with too much hostility, you're letting every tiny facet of work get under your skin, and you're freaking people out. Put aside that America hates assertive/ aggressive/ambitious women more than it hates puppy killers; put aside that if you were a man, these "problems" would most likely never have been a concern. The fact that all your performance reviews say "difficult," "rubs people the wrong way," "bedside manner: meh" cannot be blamed entirely on misogyny. This is not the case for everyone, but it is for you. You need to slow your roll just a bit, find the middle of your dial, take the time to pause, read the room, think it out, and come at the issue calmly, with a plan. By not doing this, you're hurting yourself more than you're hurting anyone else.

Stop Treating Your Career Like a Race to the Death Sprint

Man alive, you are going to put so many hours into this career, so many weekends and early mornings and late nights. You are going to talk about this career until you're hoarse, and work so hard you feel blind. You need to slow down; it's not going anywhere. You need to take care of yourself. Stop drinking so much. Get some sleep. Sit for a moment with your disappointments instead of racing to the next thing. Stop trying to run away from uncomfortable situations. Identify your triggers; understand what makes you feel most anxious and insecure, so your anxiety and insecurity don't make you do fucked-up things to other people. Read all those old *New Yorkers*. Or don't. Read a trashy book. Or better, read Cheryl Strayed. Just read something that has nothing to do with your job. Stop hoarding your vacation days. They're not going to fire you, at least not for taking a vacation. Take advantage of the health care plan you don't understand that costs you $7,995 a month and get yourself some therapy. You need it. Needing it doesn't make you a freak. Go to the gym. Or take a walk. Do something active with your limbs. Spend two hours a day not thinking about work. Don't eat four pieces of toast and a block of cheese before bed unless you want to wake up feeling like you ate four pieces of toast and a block of cheese. When all else fails, do a face mask. It's going to be OK. You're weird, sure, but you're better than you think. Sometimes you're even great.

PART III
Weird in
the World

CHAPTER 13
That #Boss Life

Most of us don't get proper training on how to be a good boss. We get a promotion one day, or we start our own business, and suddenly, *POOF*, we're managers, in charge of the majority of another person's time, her livelihood, the thing that, by the numbers at least, she puts more energy into than any other part of her life.

The "idea" of being a boss is discussed all the time. It's become a sort of cultural trope, a social media lingua franca, an anthem for power and empowerment. Our virtual lives are bursting with hashtags—#likeaboss #bossbitch #bossbabe #bossedup—meant to convey our dominance, our authority, our financial superiority, our support for other women who impressively hold sway over their personal domain and mastery over their careers, who've achieved an exalted level of success, upon which we all agree. When we talk about female bosses, it's an online cheer, almost a jingle. It's a fast nod and a slow clap of solidarity. In a world where female leaders are still woefully undervalued, underemployed, and underrepresented in almost every vocation—where, once they arrive, they're overscrutinized and disproportionately criticized; where we're still wary and dismissive of and even repelled by female ambition; where women represent only 4 percent of CEOs, direct only 7 percent of all films, and hold only 19 percent of the seats in the House and Senate combined— this rally cry, this #girlboss communion, has critical value in changing the perception of what a woman can and cannot be. It's essential to our collective success.

But it doesn't help you become a good boss.

And you'd be hard-pressed to find models for great female bosses in popular culture. Instead we're presented with insensitive, impenetrable boss-bots like Miranda Priestly in *The Devil Wears Prada*, Wilhelmina Slater on the series *Ugly Betty*, or Tilda Swinton's Dianna in *Trainwreck*. Or modern-day psychotraumatists like Quinn on *Unreal*—women who are incredible at their jobs at incredible cost to everyone else. The flip side is fluffy (but entertaining and hilarious) female bosses on shows like *The Mindy Project*, more interested in gossip and clothes than the business or their employees' lives; ineffectual neurotics like *30 Rock's* Liz Lemon, who, as wonderful and relatable and forever GIF-able she is, is still unable to rule her unruly roost.* Hollywood has overwhelmingly presented us with a binary for how women in business behave: you are hapless or you are monstrous; you need someone to save you, or you should be shown the door.

The formative career movies of my youth were no better

---

* There's at least one exception to the rule here: Amy Poehler's unapologetically ambitious, hardworking, lovable weirdo Leslie Knope on *Parks and Rec*, particularly her unflinching support for other women and her compassionate mentorship of April.

at showing boss role models. Rose, from *Don't Tell Mom the Babysitter's Dead* (a surprisingly astute and inspiring film about ambition, the workplace, and '80s fashion, despite what the name suggests), is a warm, kindly manager who's— seemingly—competent at her job but still lacks self-awareness and confidence, and becomes too distracted by takeout lunches, flower deliveries, and her relationship with a smarmy coworker to save the failing business in her charge. When the chips are down, she helplessly clutches an oversize jar of Good & Plenties and awaits a bailout from her seventeen-year-old assistant, Christina Applegate's transcendent Sue Ellen.

In *Baby Boom*, a movie that opens with a documentary-style homage to the 1980s working woman and all she can achieve, Diane Keaton's smart, strong, supremely talented lawyer J. C. Wiatt is so upended by new motherhood that she allows a back-stabbing male underling, a protégé she *found* and *trained*, to unseat her from the firm's biggest case. She is left to flee to Vermont and make applesauce for a living, though we're supposed to buy that it's all worth it for a few makeout sessions with rural doc Sam Shepard.

Even my favorite career movie of all time, *Working Girl*, a film I've watched approximately 452 times, represents women in power as little more than heartless and scheming, a dragon-lady-in-shoulder-pads archetype. Sigourney Weaver's Katherine Parker is a tormenter who uses other women, and uses her sexuality to play men and get ahead. She manipulates her hardworking, beatific assistant Tess McGill (our heroine), exploits her trust and desire for mentorship, and steals her ideas. In the movie's last scene, when a triumphant Tess has overcome Katherine, when she's finally made it and is sitting in her new Manhattan office with the *Let the River Run* view, we get a glimpse of how Tess will go on to be the supportive, nurturing, tough-but-fair boss of all our dreams, but we never see her do it.

This makes sense, of course. The reason we rarely see great female leadership on film is because the world is sexist,* and as a society, we haven't sorted out how to view believably powerful women without overemphasizing their flaws and explaining ad nauseam how they're specially fucked up. As a result, Hollywood has yet to discover how to portray inspiring, not-fucked-up boss role models outside of noble-stoic male characters and, particularly, coaches (are there any cozier and more American metaphors for winning at life than winning at sports?).

In fact, pop culture is teeming with male-on-male mentorship, especially in movies, across genres: Dicky Fox in *Jerry Maguire*, Mister X in *X-Men*, Mr. Miyagi in *Karate Kid*, Obi-Wan Kenobi in the *Star Wars* movies (the ones where he's not dead), Lester Bangs in *Almost Famous*, Mickey Goldmill in *Rocky*, Morgan Freeman as Somerset in *Se7en* (but also Morgan Freeman in a million other movies)—all overwhelmingly wise and mostly kind Y-chromosome characters teaching other Ys how to be good at what they do. By contrast, few films depict female mentorship/bossing in the same light; if you take away teachers, nuns, and sex workers, there are essentially zero. It's as if we're afraid that if we show women as positive business role models (who are not teachers or nuns or sex workers), women will actually think they can be good at business.

Beyond obvious sexism, the reason Hollywood rarely depicts

---

* Obviously.

the nitty-gritty of great female leadership, of setting goals and addressing employee gripes, of giving productive feedback and incentivizing a team of humans to perform and collaborate, is because being a good leader isn't actually all that glamorous, exciting, or entertaining. It's not all ass-smacking Coach Taylor "Clear Eyes, Full Hearts, Can't Lose" triumph. Managing is stultifying and time-consuming. Doing it well can be tedious and frustrating; it's a critical part of the job, but it's often thankless and selfless. And a big reason that we don't see more positive portrayals of great bosses is because, honestly, most people aren't that good at it.

I am wary to wade in here. There are *experts*, very serious people with PhDs in human behavior and human brains, who've written about this at length, who have devoted their lives to the study of leadership and what motivates people to perform. There are entire library sections and bookstore shelves devoted to advice on how good leaders should eat, dress, think, talk, dare, influence, communicate, innovate, ideate, motivate—all the -ates. There are groundbreaking books on the habits of world-famous CEOs, coaches, dictators, icons, trailblazers in their fields, and how to emulate those habits. These books get people stoked to do great things; they teach the secret formula for managerial success, albeit often in a one-size-fits-all way.

Like any ambitious go-getter seeking her fortune in the new world, I've read many of these leadership books. I've had take-charge TODAY IS THE DAY I GET MY SHIT TOGETHER moments, headed to the nearest bookstore (Amazon/my couch), and bought stacks at a time. I've piled them up on my night-stand, skimmed them over, highlighted one or two paragraphs with a neon-orange highlighter, and then fallen asleep with them on my chest, as if the information could be gleaned through osmosis, as if just by owning them I would be transformed. I've found these books months later under my bed, among dust bunnies and old sports bras, abandoned running shoes, batteries, bobby pins, lost work-shirt buttons; the detritus of trying to live my best life, the materials for a MacGyver bomb.

These books are *important*; they have good intentions and bring smart information to the world. They are big books with big ideas. But I've seen too many managers hide behind these big books and their big ideas, as if reading these books, studying their project-management flow charts and their employee-satisfaction stats, and memorizing their italicized crisis-management and team-building anecdotes made those managers experts on how to deal with actual human beings in a humane way.

I've watched mediocre men and out-of-touch women quote from these books, telling me what *drives* employees, because they know, because they read the book—and then, in the same breath, make tone-deaf, morale-crushing, ass-stupid decisions about restructuring, about terminations, about changes in direction that affected people's lives in profoundly negative ways; decisions that came about under the guise of a big leadership ideology, but were, behind the curtain, really about that manager's shortcomings, about unchecked ego and general ineptitude.

The hidden message in these books seems to be that, to be a great boss, you must be a paragon of stability. You're supposed to have transcended your awkwardness and anxiety, and simplified the human condition into a series of colors, charts, surveys, reports—the forensics of a PowerPoint slide. You're not supposed to feel too much, just enough to not seem like a droid. But this is a limiting myth. Feelings are what will get you through this. If you want to be a great boss, your weirdness and sensitivity can translate into inspiring leadership that has tremendous meaning, that changes the course of other peoples' lives and your own in the process. First, you're going to make mistakes.

Here to Make Friends

The first time I was ever an official boss, one with significant boss responsibilities, was at the big tech company where I'd been initially hired as a fashion and beauty blogger. I'd signed on in a more junior position than the one I'd had at the fashion magazine—the money was better, and I was eager to make the move from print to digital—but within a year, I was promoted to an in-office job as deputy editor of the site. The tech company was more corporate and formal than anyplace I'd ever worked before; it took management and chain of command *seriously*. When they made you a manager, you were crowned with a manager checkmark next to your name in the corporate system, the nuclear codes for firing someone, a barrage of red tape and inefficient protocols that got in the way of your doing your job, and a list of humans under you on the organizational chart/company family tree. I was promoted from within, and at the same time I inherited a team. This meant that I was now in charge of people I had not hired and who, for several months, had been my peers. This meant an uphill battle to gain respect in a new position of authority. In other words, I was essentially—unless I knew how to play my cards right, and at the time I did not even understand what those cards were—fucked.

The team I was managing had (mostly) all started together. We were a bicoastal team of writers and editors hired to launch a women's website within an enormous, deeply troubled 1.0 tech company struggling to define its identity in a 2.0 world. In the months since our launch, we'd borne out our promise, establishing "proof of concept": a large portion of the company's extraordinarily large readership were women (go figure!) who wanted to read about lifestyle topics—food, parenting, health, style, relationships, work—through a female lens.* We were meeting and exceeding our aggressive quarterly goals. Advertisers loved us; we were making the company millions already that year. We were the number one site in our category, with 40 million readers a month, easily beating our biggest competitors, media companies who were long established in the space. We had a lean, scrappy (mostly), innovative team, and ran our siloed operation like a start-up, finding nimble solutions to problems other groups within the company were never able to solve. By any measure of corporate success, we were successful.

On paper, everything looked GREAT at the site I worked for—if I had entered this situation as a new hire, I would have been thrilled. But because I'd been in the trenches and was an established employee, I knew there were serious problems lurking under this shiny surface. For one, the company's in-

---

* This formula had worked for women's magazines for decades, and it worked for us too.

ternal culture—despite a rah-rah umbrella of support and
unity, of ropes courses and company cheers—was hostile and
competitive, a disorganized bureaucracy, a dog-eat-dog race for
budget and resources, support, and distribution, all of which
overwhelmingly went to middling company men doing middling, often archaic company work. At that time, our site and
the work of our all-female staff was denigrated by the people in
charge. The general consensus was that we were doing fluffy
chick shit. We were deprioritized, and every improvement or
extra resource was hard-won.

Despite a handful of strong female leaders, the company
culture was overwhelmingly masculine. The parts of the business most revered and given highest priority were traditional
male things—sports and finance, things that produced stories
that male executives were interested in reading, that they understood. In my first meeting with the male vice president of
content, after remarking on how many members of my team
were pregnant (two), he suggested I get more "nip slips" on the
page. "That really clicks!" he explained. It was the only direct
editorial guidance I ever received.

After months working in these conditions, the staff was unruly and uneven, demoralized and burned out. Our daily work-
flow was inefficient, our tools were difficult to use, our roles ill
defined, our goals unclear. We were all regularly pulled into
nonsensical meetings that ate up hours of the day. The distribution of work was tilted heavily toward the strongest employees. Resentment was boiling over. Under the surface, it was a
mess.

After my promotion, it became, at least in part, my mess.

The staff was an even three-way split: a third were excellent, a third were underdeveloped with real potential, and the final third were . . . problematic. As the rotting-apples cliché goes, that last third was dragging everyone down. They were whining the loudest, complaining the most. They interrupted important meetings to air personal grievances and spread baseless gossip throughout the day. They did not want to work for me; they probably didn't even want to work there. And they were fundamentally mediocre at their jobs.

It's difficult to establish your authority when you become a leader in a team of which you've been a longtime member. The staff still saw me as a peer, not a boss. They remembered when we got drunk on the company retreat and talked about how I thought that guy from sales was hot. Now I was attempting to CHANGE RULES and ENFORCE things. Now I was attempting to HOLD THEM ACCOUNTABLE. Now I was a buzz kill.

Instead of doing the two things I have learned are more important than anything else in management—1. Be as honest and straightforward as you possibly can, whenever you can, and 2. Address all toxic behavior immediately and nip petty bullshit situations in the bud—I coddled. I was overly empathetic and nurturing. Imagining that this would inspire loyalty, I listened to their gripes, daily, to the point that it took up time when I should have been focusing on my job. I exacerbated the performance issues by allowing these employees to believe their own hype, to believe they were doing satisfactory work, when they were not. When I couldn't motivate them to complete projects up to my standard, I completed them myself. I covered for them with the rest of the team. I defended them to higher-ups who asked if they were the "weak links." I wanted to love them, and I desperately wanted to be liked. I was there to make friends. Because I did not address troubling issues with the severity they deserved and because of the fascinating brain chemistry that makes some people think they are great despite overwhelming evidence to the contrary, while the rest of us continuously believe we are a human form of that fake-beef pink slime, I exacerbated the problem. This led to months of infighting, HR meetings, and staff turmoil, and, finally, a cinematic-level resignation.

One of my employees was particularly difficult. She repeatedly blew off deadlines; at least once she published a story that was not true, and another time she published a story that was partially plagiarized. After a few drinks at a work event, she approached my boss and told him I didn't care about her or the other employees, that they "all" thought I should be replaced. The conversation got back to me. Instead of doing what I wanted to—turn into the Hulk and scream "HULK MAD!," a strategy that would have been satisfying in the moment but would not have produced anything close to results—I decided to stop being nice. The next week, once the sting had worn off and I was sure I could be cool, I set up a meeting and calmly addressed the employee's performance issues. But it was too late; I'd let it go on too long. She thought the world was flat, and I was telling her it was round. Her response was to yell, "I AM NOT A DERELICT. YOU ARE TREATING ME LIKE A DERELICT. I WILL NOT BE TREATED LIKE A DERELICT!," and then storm out of the room we were sitting in, march to her cube, and begin dramatically packing her things, throwing them higher than they needed to be thrown, banging things harder than they needed to be banged—all to desired attention and stares. For the next hour, she whispered with other employees in office corners. She cried in the bathroom. I had to call security. I had to collect all of her company-owned things. I had to accept that the situation was actually happening and that it was, at least in part, my fault. Before her computer was confiscated, she sent a dramatic good-bye e-mail to the staff and simultaneously blocked me from all of her social media accounts.

Making friends, indeed.

I fumbled a great deal during those first few years of management. I made all the rookie boss mistakes: I promised too much and gave too little; I unintentionally contradicted myself and gave inconsistent, unclear direction; I was too hopeful and too open; I had unrealistic expectations, made assumptions, and projected my feelings onto others; I expected employees to read my mind. But I wanted to get better. And I tried hard to get better. It was as important to me as anything else I'd ever done. And here is probably the hardest sentence I will write in this entire book, because honestly I'd rather tell you about my failed first marriage or copious underarm sweat than own my talent and achievement, but here goes:

Over the years, I've become a fucking great boss.

I am a better boss than I was a waitress, student, assistant, fact-checker, even an editor and writer. As bad as I am at keeping houseplants alive (read: even cacti stand no chance), I am that good at helping humans do their best work. The degree to which I am unable to navigate the "cells" of a spreadsheet and efficiently update my Adobe Flash is only surpassed by my ability to zero in on an employee's strengths and help her identify and fulfill her dreams. My oddness, my hypersensitivity, my ambition, the fact that I've lived a full, fucked-up life—all of this, the sum of my unique parts, has made me the kind of boss I always wanted, one who creates the type of professional environments I'd always wanted to work in, compassionate meritocracies where honesty and empathy are paramount, where expectations are clearly set, and where, as an employee, you feel supported and always know where you stand.

This doesn't mean I always like managing, nor that I find it easy—it can actually be exhausting, a giant pain in the ass. And I certainly make mistakes to this day. But if the thesis of this book is that work is more intimate and emotional for us hypersensitive weirdos, becoming great at managing other people has been *the* most intimate and emotional part of working for me, one of the hardest things I've ever had to do. It's also been the most rewarding. Because thinking about the success of other human beings made me much more chill about my own.

My ideas about leadership are simple. They are the Cliffs-Notes, Managing for Weirdos 101. They start with giving a damn, with taking the responsibility of being a boss seriously, no matter how small your project or team, with taking accountability for your actions—and always, every day, even when you don't feel like it, even when you would rather be hiding and eating an entire, not-defrosted frozen cheesecake under your desk with an old takeout spork you fished out of a drawer, even then, still showing up and trying your best.

My management philosophy was born out of the idea that because I'd been given so much, because in my hardest, most lost and loser-feeling times, someone, whether a boss or not, had swooped in with encouragement and kindness, it was my duty to give this kindness back. And because I'd spent my life secretly or not-so-secretly feeling awkward, odd, and misunderstood—and, on my worst days, talentless, useless, and stupid—I did not want any talented and hardworking person who worked for me to ever feel the same.

Shiny, Happy Boundaries

Being a boss for the first time is lonelier than you imagine. You're an authority figure now, someone on whom employees can project their insecurities, doubts, company ill will, and on-the-job fear. Given your new "boss" status, you may be left out of the fun, no longer invited to last-minute coffee grabs or after-work drinks. Every interaction becomes more complicated. You will awkwardly and unknowingly shut down otherwise lighthearted Slack chats just by weighing in. Even if you make a hilarious joke, that joke has different meaning than before: no one knows whether they can laugh or not, or if they do laugh, they'll wonder if you'll think they're a kiss-ass or if everyone else will think they're a kiss-ass. Your at-work inner circle will become smaller. You may miss camaraderie; you will be excluded from cross-platform shit-talk and chitter-chatter sessions of which you were once a part and maybe even a ringleader. Now these sessions will often be about you. Depending on the health of your ego, either you will accept this new reality and be like "That's awesome, you guys have fun. It makes me happy that you're happy" or, like an aging, suburban mom unable to let go of her youth, you will awkwardly insert and insinuate yourself into your employees lives, *force* them to be your friends. You will make it weird.

As a new boss, you may want to seem cool and fun. Even if you are a paragon of self-sufficiency and emotional tidiness (which, if you've picked up this book . . .), you will probably want people to like you. This is a normal instinct for normal people in normal situations. But being a leader is not normal. There are different rules. The first is that you're going to need some good boundaries.

One of the more popular healthy-people advice clichés, one of those things you hear in conversation and see in books, the magic bullet that will solve all of your current personal and professional problems and improve relations with your boyfriend/dog/boss/employee/mom, is to just "get some good boundaries." Just *git sum*. Get some electrical tape into the fourth dimension of your soul and mark off the places that are available to people you work with and those that are not and stick that tape down strong and then everything is going to get better. Girl, you know it's true.

Even if you intellectually understand what this means, even if you get that you shouldn't be BFF with people who work for you, putting the "boundaries" advice into practice is easier said than done, particularly if you've never had to do it before, if you are watery and heartful, if you run deep with empathy and self-consciousness, if you have warm blood.

Bad boundaries are easier to define than good ones. Boundaries-lacking bosses ooze all over employees. They tell them too much, they act like peers and friends, but then, seemingly arbitrarily but really because some serious boss shit has come up, they freeze them out. You shouldn't do that. You shouldn't get in your employees' physical space, sit on their laps, show them your breasts, hug them when they don't want to be hugged.* You shouldn't tell your employees about your marriage, or conflicts with your nanny, cleaning lady, or trainer, and leave them to do nothing but mutely, awkwardly stare at you and your boss-lady problems when really they just came in to ask a question about work, one that goes unanswered because of all these bad boundaries.

Bosses who lack boundaries often have the best intentions. They're just trying to create lighthearted working environments and keep things fun, but they fail to realize that to work efficiently with a minimum of confusion, employees need structure and authority. Sometimes they need you to be the fun killer; to give an unequivocal no or a strict, plans-destroying deadline or a firm "This isn't good enough. I need you to try again." For work to actually work, someone has to be a dick, at least sometimes. And once you are a boss, you are the dick. You need to be OK with being disliked in the moment. No one makes good decisions by trying to curry favor or win approval. You need to understand that people who are mad will get glad again; you need to have perspective on the greater good.

Bosses with good boundaries are comfortable with this dick reality, and by extension they make others comfortable too. They're cool with having control (or they fake being cool) and power (and they don't abuse it). They are consistent and fair, they set rules and expectations that make employees feel safe. They don't make it all about them. They don't turn their insecurity or their narcissism or both into an interactive theater show, a daily performance of "Look at me! I need attention!,"

---

* My real-life experience may have been a tad strange, I guess?

and force everyone in their wake to participate, at the expense of actual work.

Having good boundaries as a boss means keeping yourself contained. It also means protecting yourself from employees who want to take too much from you, not internalizing things that are definitely NOT your problem, such as other people's insecurity, incompetence, laziness, jealousy, and gossip, and addressing things that are—overall morale, efficient distribution of work, clarity around expectations and goals, your own human failings and mistakes. It's ballsy work. It takes confidence you might not have at first, but you can get it.

Braveheart, Not the Movie

Trust me when I say this: bravery is the key that unlocks the door to the room where your employees' respect is hiding.

It takes bravery to be honest with someone about her performance. It takes bravery to hold other people accountable without blowing up in their faces. It takes bravery and confidence to be decisive, to set a clear path for your team with your best instincts and intentions, even if you might be wrong. It is courageous to acknowledge when it was you, not them, who fucked everything up, to own it, to apologize and move on. BE BRAVE with the people who work for you. Don't be passive-aggressive; don't give them roundabout instructions or say the opposite of what you actually want because it sounds nicer; don't expect people to read your mind and then get mad when they don't perform.

Be a working model your employees can look up to. Advocate for them, always. Don't back down from tough administrative battles, even if they are excessively complicated and annoying. Fight for your staff's earned raises and their deserved promotions, push back against thoughtless executives who try to save a buck at the expense of employee well-being, who put careless policies into place, who try to screw over junior employees who don't know any better, who offer them lowered wages and whittled-down benefits and then Disneyvillain laugh about the employees' ignorance while counting up their own company equity or SkyMiles or whatever Scrooge McDuck thing greedy-evil executives count up.

Speak out against subtle racism and overt sexism. If you see something, say something: don't stand by while your employees face any form of discrimination. Shut down inappropriate conversations about race, religion, and gender identity, about body sizes and emotional states. If you don't do this, you are sending a message that this behavior is tolerable, you are saying it's OK. I shouldn't have to explain this, I know. But these conversations happen, are still happening, have happened at every place I've worked. Even if it's not you doing the discriminating, even if you would *never* say that or do that, even if you feel guilty, if you go home and pour a big ol' glass of privilege wine and admit to your partner/roommate/pet how fucked it all is, if you are in a position of power and you stand by and let discrimination happen because you are afraid to ruffle a few feathers or challenge the status quo or you just don't feel like standing up to the company bully that day, you are complicit in the bigotry, guilty by association. You are being a coward.

Don't take advantage of your position. Even when you don't feel like it, even when it seems so easy to just fuck around, show up on time, don't nap during the office workday, don't laze out. When there's a real problem, be a leader who leads things. Don't let an issue fester and cause a viral-fear outbreak among your staff; make a decision, quickly sort out how to communicate that decision, and then get that message out. When there are difficult calls to make, make them. It takes bravery to fire people when they really need to be fired. When it's time to do this, step up. Don't run away. Don't do it over text like some sad *Sex and the City* plot. Don't make your beleaguered second-in-command, the one you're still paying an assistant's wages, do it. Be brave; your staff will respect you for it. And the trick to any of this going well, more than being feared or even loved, is to be respected.

Hiring for Winners

When I first started interviewing people, I had essentially zero idea what I was doing. I got nervous and sweaty, I was uncomfortable in my position of power, and I overcompensated by being overly formal and stiff, by following HR "talent acquisition" guidelines to a tee. This resulted in my hiring people who looked good on paper, who answered all my formulaic questions with pat, right-sounding answers, but who often turned out to be ambivalent about work and lackluster in their roles, uninspiring to work with and around. Or I accidentally chose self-serving ambition monsters who were in it for themselves, with no intention of collaborating with a team. Or humans who were ultimately too insecure and self-loathing to assert themselves and take productive feedback, the kinds of people whose unbounded self-doubt and need made my life as a manager a bag of fuck. After too many of these hiring mistakes, I now do things differently. I've learned that I am an unconventional person and an unconventional boss, and this needs to (duh) be taken into account when I interview people, because hiding who I am in an interview and how our office works will only lead to mismatches and, ultimately, an ordeal that everyone would rather avoid.

I start every interview with a story. I briefly, in less than five minutes, explain where I come from, how I came to the company where we are sitting. I tell the interviewee what makes me excited about what I do, how the company is succeeding, and, within reason, the challenges we are facing. I talk about office culture, my philosophy about managing, our mission as a team, the essentials for the position we're hiring for and why we need it filled, and what I think will happen to the company or the department in the next year. I give interviewees a fair but enthusiastic snapshot of the place they are interviewing. As best I can, I give them an intimate lay of the land. I am casual and I am honest. I close my computer; I don't check my e-mails, and I never check my phone. I maintain eye contact. I am setting a precedent in that moment for our boss-employee dynamic, how we will work together, if we work together.

Then I turn the conversation over to them, asking the first in a series of questions meant to open them up, get them jazzed about the work, and reveal who they really are: "What brought you here today?"

My goal is to upend the awkwardness of the situation, to make it less artificial, to assuage nerves and disrupt practiced

answers and polished comportment. I ask weird (but totally legal!) things. I ask people how projects or offices make them
feel. I ask what bums them out, what makes them hopeful. I
ask who they admire and if they ever wanted to be or do anything else, besides what they do now. I ask about a particular
accomplishment that made them proud. I quiz them on their
knowledge of our field and the business—which competitive brands are smartest, who is doing the best job and why. I
keep it upbeat and chatty. I let their answers go on for a long
time, sometimes more than is comfortable for everyone. And I
watch. I am watching how fast they are reacting, how quickly
they are picking up what I've put down. I watch how they talk
about themselves, how they talk about work and working and
currently wanting to make a change.

I am trying to sort out who they are in this context, how comfortable they are in their own skin, what our chemistry might
be, and how they'd fit into the team. I am trying to suss out
their judgment, to see if they are the combination of smart/
hungry/talented/funny/fundamentally kind that comes in all
forms and backgrounds but is ultimately my dream employee.

Then, when it's over, after they've asked me questions, and
from those questions and their general demeanor I can sense
their level of enthusiasm over this odd interview or desire to
run the fuck away, I offer them an assignment.

I tailor what I want to the specific position—editing tests,
audience development plans, big idea memos, tweeting without typos, etc. I give the candidate a week to complete it, though
the most ambitious turn it in earlier. Between the answers I get
from these "tests," the notes I take in interviews, and the way

they conduct themselves post-interview, the best choice usually emerges.

It doesn't always work, it's not foolproof, but I give interviewing my all, and each time it's better than it was before.

A final note on hiring: if you are living in the times we live in and not intentionally recruiting and hiring women and people of color, people who don't look like you, who don't come from where you come from, to create balanced office environments with a wide range of perspectives and diverse points of view, I honestly don't know what you're doing.

How to Give Critical Feedback and Not Sound Like a Creep

Your staff needs to know what you like, what you don't, whether they're headed in the right direction or definitely NOT headed in the right direction, and they need this information transmitted in a productive, clear, calm, coherent way that isn't passive-aggressive or aggressive-aggressive. Almost all employees are hungry for feedback. Giving it thoughtfully is time-consuming, but not when you consider the alterative: miscommunication and misunderstanding, blown deadlines and hurt feelings, losing good employees and producing mediocre work. When you think about it in these terms, as an investment that saves future-you hassles and proximity to tears, early feedback will become one of your most highly prioritized to-do items, perhaps even something you like to do.

Because receiving critical feedback makes even extremely secure employees freak out a little bit, it has to be executed

carefully to be effective. In other words, there is a compassionate way to be honest. You're allowed to lead with empathy, and
when you can, you should. Here's how.

I. If at all possible, schedule all feedback meetings at a reasonable time in the other person's day—not first thing Monday
morning, when she is trying to catch up, not when she is on
deadline, not at the drop-end of the day, when she is trying to
get home. You want your employee as present, open, and chill
as possible.

When you schedule your meeting, be considerate; make the
messaging upbeat and nonmenacing. Don't, for example, send
invites with subject lines like "Need to talk by EOD," which
will play over and over in your employee's mind like the *Jaws*
soundtrack on repeat. Don't send a request for a meeting on
Monday morning, with no context, late on a Friday afternoon,
unless you are a sadist, intentionally trying to send your employee on a weekend-long panic tour, during which she will
become sure she's going to be fired, because everyone always
thinks they're going to be fired.

DON'T TALK LIKE THIS!!! Don't be terrible and the worst
like this!

When you have to send feedback over e-mail, write a first
draft and then strip out all inflammatory and hyperbolic language in addition to all adjectives; see if the message still reads.
It probably does. Also: never use all caps. This might seem like
advice you'd give a monkey, but you'd be surprised how many
monkey managers send e-mails that include all caps, the literal translation of which is someone screaming THIS IS CRAP
AND YOU ARE SUCKY.

2. Know what you want to say and get to the point straight-

away. Start the conversation off with "I want to talk about what happened in Friday's meeting." Or "Thanks so much for sending me the presentation for Tuesday. I have some ideas for how we can make it better together." Or "It seems like there's been some miscommunication between us. I'd like to clear it up." (All of these topics suck, obviously, but, hey, this whole thing kind of sucks. Sorry!)

Don't meander in conversation or stumble around; don't eat up the meeting making nicey-nice please-still-like-me small talk; don't discuss how you're feeling about your new haircut for eleven minutes. Being generous in this context means being direct—any delays are unnecessary and cruel, forcing an already nervous employee to guess at wtf is actually happening. Remember again that everyone hates feeling like they're "in trouble," and always thinks they're about to be fired, basically all of the time. Unless you are in fact firing them, alleviate this fear straight away.

3. Point out the positives first. Sometimes they are hard to find, but still find them. Talk about initiative, talk about progress, talk about a good idea someone had or how people love working with him. If an employee has been with you for a while, highlight his growth if you can: "A year ago you were doing X, and now you're already doing Y—that's impressive and great."

4. Say "We're in this together," and mean it. Establish up front that you are there to support the employee and help her, that you care and want her to get better. Mention one of those inspiring clichés people say all the time, like "A rising tide lifts all ships." Or don't, but say something that makes her feel your support, strongly.

5. Even if you are in a rush, even if you would like to run away from this conversation because every word makes you feel more like you're the grease in a grease fire, give the employee time to let the feedback sink in. Sit in silence if you have to. Pause to say things like "Don't worry," "You totally have this!" "Do you have any questions?" "I think we can make this project/you working here even more amazing."

6. Chances are, you're not fixing everything today. Human beings can only hear so much criticism at once. Don't roll out a scroll of complaints, a rap sheet detailing each of the employee's flaws. Pick the most urgent things, specific examples of problematic work that encapsulate behavior trends, and address those head-on. If you are an editor working through a challenging story edit, let the writer have one or two things that you don't love but that are meaningful to her and ultimately don't affect the quality of the work. If you are not an editor, apply this philosophy to whatever work you do. Let the graphic designer keep one flourish or color choice that makes her feel proud and doesn't cause your eyes physical pain; let the events person keep the swag he likes so much but you think is twee, if it won't matter in the long run. Give employees something that is theirs.

7. Remember that you are speaking to another human with feelings, that your ego doesn't win anything by being "right," that engaging in a battle of wills at this juncture serves no one. Remember that receiving criticism, even the gentlest and most kindhearted, is hard for most of us non-robots, and by giving this criticism you've most likely set off an explosion of complicated emotions in the other person's brain. Know that you cannot control that person's reaction, that even if she is defensive

and pissed, even if she shuts down, it doesn't mean the whole thing backfired and that you failed. Assume that you both have the same goal to make things the best they can be, and keep focused on shepherding them there.

8. After the conversation is over, practice some self-care. Go for a walk, call someone you love, get a drink, cry. It takes real energy to give to another person, to confront a problem calmly and carefully. It takes it out of you. It can be worse if the person or thing is terrible, but giving feedback is hard anytime and always. That's why so many bosses avoid it. But not you! Be proud of yourself; you had the courage and the sensitivity to do something that made you feel uncomfortable. And you executed it thoughtfully, with kindness. Even if you feel exhausted now, you've just invested in both another person and your own future. Over time, conducting yourself like this is going to pay back in ways you can't even imagine.

Boss versus Figurehead: You Decide

We live in a new land where new businesses are built on the backs of personal brands, where one day you are a semi-famous actress out and about actressing, and the next you are president of the world's biggest artisanal bike manufacturer. Where you sat in your studio apartment, writing some smart tweets, and before you knew it, someone DM'd to offer you the top-dog position at a major media brand. Or maybe your YouTube videos became a skincare empire, your cat pics led to a cat sweater company, your popular podcast about golf made you CEO of Golf Love Dot Com, or you were a reality TV star who became president of the most powerful nation in the world. Success trajectory is faster and weirder than ever before. Anything can happen with a few thousand social media followers. You can work hard at building a relevant digital self, and in what seems like an instant, that digital self expands and morphs into a bona fide business with bona fide rules and expenses and people to manage and pay. You can become a boss without ever having had a boss. It's whiplash, it's magic, it's more complicated and stressful than you imagined.

In the interest of focus and brevity and because I know next to nothing about the topic and don't want to sound like an arse, I am not talking about what goes into being a good entrepreneur here. I believe it is some combination of grit and instinct and vision and timing and being able to appear like an actual capable human and not an eager, too-thirsty Labrador retriever in women's business clothing, but I am not entirely sure. What I do know is what it takes to be a boss, and if you are an entrepreneur who has come to be in charge of your own humans-employing brand, at some point you are going to have to make an important decision. Are you an in-the-trenches boss or are you a figurehead boss?

Because here's the truth: your proximity to celebrity does not make you a good boss. Neither does having a lot of money or fame. Nor your social media imprint, no matter how impressive it may be. You will gain surface admiration for these things, you will initially become a projection of employees' fantasies and #goals, but if you don't actually do the work of managing, if you hate it and it makes you cagey and strange, if you resent and just don't *wanna* do it but insist on doing it because your ego says you should be in charge of all things, you are going to be extremely frustrated and unhappy with your new enterprise, and your business is going to be a shitpit for anyone who works there.

Being a boss isn't about glory or accolades, the public-facing perks, the company credit cards and the prestigious business cards, the fancy LinkedIn profile and sending out some tweets. Being a boss isn't a persona, it's a J-O-B with serious responsibilities and a deep level of obligation to other humans. You are not #bossedup if you cower in the face of calamity, if you are reduced to tantrums when it all gets too hard—even though these are often totally natural reactions to the nonsense being flung your way. Being a boss means having the courage to sit in discomfort, to allow yourself to be on display and say the hard things that no one else wants to say, to plan ahead, to do grown-up things that suck. And you might not want to do these things; you might not want to spend your one God-given life refereeing mind-numbing squabbles, delivering performance reviews, and talking about quarterly goals. This instinct is understandable, it's normal, it is totally OK. It does not make you less. You may want to just be the personal brand you were born to be, out personal-branding. If you are in a position of running something, a big something or a small something, if you find yourself the biggest C in the C-suite, but you are not actually interested in the work of leading, that's OK too. Your success strategy here is simple: all you need to do is put your ego aside, be secure and mature enough to hire someone else to do the actual work of bossing, know yourself and your strengths well enough to empower a competent person, and trust and get out of that person's way. Don't pop in occasionally and pop off aggressively about situations you don't understand because you want everyone to remember who you are. They do remember. Don't terrorize your workers intermittently because you're afraid you don't have enough power. You do have power and you do have value, and part of being powerful is knowing when to back off and shut the fuck up because the situation doesn't need you.

If you don't want to commit to, or genuinely don't have the time for, consistent daily leadership and nitty-gritty involvement in the working day, then you want to be a figurehead boss, not a boss-boss. That's cool. That's honest. This honesty will make for a happy, productive, functional company. This is how you will succeed. You will rely on smart people, you will advise and influence your highest-ranking employees, and you will keep yourself engaged by expanding your company in the areas in which you truly excel: big-picture vision, marketing, creativity, glad-handing, being out in the world, cheerleading for your company and its success. You will have a great life doing what you are very good at, which is being you. THERE IS NOTHING WRONG WITH THIS. Not everyone can do it. You will come to meetings sporadically to great fanfare and send your employees treats to boost morale. You will be beloved, mythical, and successful. You will be everything you ever wanted to be.

CHAPTER 14

Check Yourself

was on a conference call the day I realized I was becoming a jerk. Because every conference call line in America sounds like voices projected through tin cans in a wind machine and/or glass shards spinning inside a rock tumbler, there was static and a weird echo on the call, so you heard what everyone said twice. When it was my turn to talk, the voice coming back at me was hard and tight. I cut people off, lobbed accusations, singled a person out harshly for something that was not entirely her fault, was more agitated and impatient than the situation required. In short, I sounded—at least in this one echoing conversation—like an asshole.

This wasn't a complete surprise. I'd been fighting it out for months in a precarious job situation, coupled with personal challenges that had taken a toll. I was overwhelmed and unmoored, buckling under the weight of new obligations and responsibility and next-level adultness along with heightened scrutiny from my family, bosses, and peers. Oh, and I had a new baby. And a broken arm. And I'd just lost my house. Still, I didn't like what I heard.

But let me back up a bit. At some point in my life, I went to a hospital and delivered a human baby whom I wanted desperately and whom I loved cosmically. The fact that I pushed this baby I love out of my body does not mean we are about to enter into the "having it all" section of this book. That phrase is a flaming pile of sexist poo that we should all excise from our memories forever, along with guilt, shame, and the plot of the Human Centipede movie(s). It's important to me to separate the fact that I am a mom from the fact that I am a boss, in this book and in my life. I don't want to be asked how I juggle it all. I don't juggle, I cry. Motherhood isn't a circus act. I try my best. Sometimes it all seems OK and like the wheels are staying on the bus, and other times it doesn't and, once alone in a confined space, I staccato-scream "FUCK! FUCK! FUCK!" as loudly as my lung capacity will allow.

I have a partner who does his share of the work of parenting and the work of living, as he should, as he should without a pat on the back, without being treated like his "support" of me and of our family is a revelation or a gift, like he is a magical elf sent from the Island of Good Men Who Give a Damn. He does his share of the work because it's his job as much as it is mine, and because once you fertilize an egg with your man-sperm and that egg grows into a kid who breathes oxygen on Earth, being a present dad is a moral imperative, not a nice-to-have. My husband works too. He is smart and talented and he gets good jobs. No one in all the jobs he's had since our kid was born has ever asked him about fatherhood and how he manages. Neither of us has it all. We have some, at different times, and we take what we can get.

On the morning after I returned from maternity leave after having my human baby, my big boss at the big tech company

called. It was eight in the morning, she was chirpy and excited, she had news. She was leaving, to go back to magazines,
actually—she was resigning that day. She expected there would
be press around the announcement. The magazine where she
was going was popular and well known, there was intrigue,
someone was getting fired, it was a juicy media story. Could I
please make sure the site's home page looked presentable? A lot
of people would be looking it.

After we hung up, because I am nothing if not conscien-
tious and also sometimes a terrible delegator, I reprogrammed
every story and every module on our site's front page. I made
the home page look presentable as requested—clever headlines
and compelling images! Yeah!—I top-edited a 2010 hot take on
either Taylor Momsen or Levi Johnston or Mel Gibson or sugar
tits, I don't remember, and then I lowered my body slowly to the
floor and entered into a full-blown panic.

There are few times in a woman's career, or at least in my
career up until that point, when you feel more vulnerable than
the first weeks coming back from maternity leave. Having a
baby is a (beautiful, life-affirming, yadda) cataclysm, one that
permanently reorders your physical makeup, your priorities,
and even your values. I could not conceive of how business
me was going to coexist with new-mom me. After weeks spent
cooin' and cuddlin' and keepin' an infant alive, I'd grown soft.
I was weepy and milky. My breasts were a science experiment
I had not mastered—intermittently rock-hard or spewing milk,
always throbbing. I carried around a ten-pound device that
extracted fluid from the two spouts on my chest as if I were
bovine. The day before my boss called and announced her resignation, my first day back on the job, I dropped my tiny person

off at her new day care, handed over her tiny personal effects, and walked out stoically. Then I stood on the sidewalk and wept until my body rocked. *She was so little how could I leave her oh my God how would this all work.* My head was not, as they say, in the game.

I'd been in business long enough to know that when a big boss leaves a giant, matrixed corporation, when a chess piece has been removed from the board, almost anything can happen. Executives at the highest level, unfamiliar with the ins and outs of the daily work, can change big-picture direction; projects that you've been working on for months can be abandoned; entire departments can be shuttered. If a new boss doesn't understand the team and what they do, if she's been kicking around the company for years waiting for a chance to put her personal stamp on something, to shake things up and make them over in her name, if she is not that good, if styles and personalities clash—you could easily lose your job, or your job could become a hellfire overnight.

So it mattered little if my head was in this game or back at home sitting on my My Brest Friend cushion and catching feelings over Sophie the Giraffe. This was my new reality, and I had to live in it, and I had to win at it. I couldn't lose my job. As I saw it, the only way to control the chaos was to lean way the fuck in and try to get my boss's job. I was the deputy editor of our website, and she was the editor in chief; it was just one step. It seemed logical, if gag-inducingly terrifying, that I could, by will and sheer force, make it happen. The day she quit, after lying on the floor and visualizing a breezy, pastoral scene, I got up and made a list of all the people within the company I needed to contact. I contacted them, one by one, on the phone. I stated my intentions—"I would like this position, how can I get it, thankyouverymuch." I pleaded my case. I leaned on my company allies, I leaned on my good reputation. By the end of the week I was "interim editor in chief" in a "trial period." It was a start.

As "interim editor in chief," my first task was to act like I knew what I was doing, which I did not, at least not enough, to be sure. Since a blazer is still the universal symbol that a female means business, I took to wearing one every day, over everything. I scheduled official meetings in the official meetings scheduler. I sent important e-mails and titled them important things like "Checking in" and "Some thoughts." In the first week back, I got completely caught up on goals, budgets, metrics, and any shifts in the company strategy I'd missed when I was gone. I parroted phrases I'd heard in meetings but up until that point had never uttered. I told people we had to get our "ducks in a row." I suggested I would like to "move the needle." I wondered aloud what we needed to "utilize" and "leverage." I asked people to "take this offline." I made Very Important PowerPoint Presentations and presented them to Very Important People. I put on a big-boss mask and hoped I passed as a big boss.

But there were cracks in my facade. One morning I forgot my pump and had to sit through four hours of back-to-back meetings, my breasts growing fuller and more painful, toilet paper tucked into my bra. Toward the end of the day I was recapping a conversation with a male colleague, standing at the whiteboard, when I felt a weird, wet sensation. I looked down and saw milk not just leaking, but *bubbling* through my shirt. I was a human breast-milk fountain standing in a fluorescent-lit conference room.

The next week, after dropping my daughter off on a rainy morning and racing to the subway to make an important appointment (with an advertiser who had the potential to bring millions to our site), I slipped on the sidewalk. The weight of my pump, laptop bag, and purse, all slung over one shoulder, disabled my shaky-in-the-best-of-circumstances balance. I broke my fall not with a steady palm, but with my elbow. It shattered upon contact. I required surgery—four pins and two plates, not quite enough metal to set off airport security alarms, just enough to feel slightly bionic. I could not type with my right hand for weeks.

Later that month our landlord, a benevolent old lady who loved dogs and flowers and us, decided to cash in on Brooklyn's real estate boom, sell her beautiful old brownstone, and live out her days with her dogs in a condo in Belize. The buyers would be converting the multi-apartment space into their own design-y single-family dwelling. Our decade-long rent-control deal was done. We had to move. After a weeks-long search, marching around Brooklyn in an arm sling and with an infant, the closest habitable option we could barely afford was farther from work, farther from child care, and more than double what we were paying before.

Next came bad luck of our own making: my husband was offered and accepted an exciting new position, a yearlong contract that came with a convoluted, irregular, and not-guaranteed pay schedule, something we'd completely overlooked in our enthusiasm for the upward movement of the role. (There are many strengths in our partnership, but money management is not one of them; combined, we have the financial acumen of a not-excelling-at-math second-grader, or, more accurately, a sieve.)

Now we were essentially a one-income household, with a 60 percent increase in rent. After the moving costs and out-of-pocket hospital bills for my arm, we had next to zero savings. We had a baby and her attendant survival and child-care costs. We borrowed money and fell into debt. We had lamps propped atop unpacked moving boxes because we couldn't afford furniture. It was winter, and the closest subway station to our new apartment shut down for repairs. Like ancient grandpas in olden days telling tales of woe, we walked a mile to get to day care each day, uphill one way, in the snow.

And I still had the "interim editor in chief" situation to contend with.

I began to self-isolate. I was too miserable and embarrassed by our situation to talk to friends. My arm would not bend all the way, which made me feel even more self-conscious than usual, and I was on display more than ever—in meetings, in presentations, with strangers. I was working full office days and then coming home and putting in hours more at home. I was working more hours, doing higher-level tasks, for the same money that I'd made before.

Months went by like this. I had made zero progress with the big tech company; there was no clarity about my title changing from "interim" to "real." There was no talk of more money. I was stressed, and I was increasingly pissed. This wasn't the kind of anger that helps you get things done; this was the seed of paralyzing bitterness and resentment that blocks any path to future success.

So I did the thing most of us do in situations that bring us discomfort: I tried to escape. I looked for other jobs. I was up for senior positions now, but there were fewer of them. The ones I was actually interested in were harder to get. I sailed through six interviews for an editor-in-chief position I wanted at a website I liked, then lost in the final round, when it was head-to-head between me and another candidate. I blew it in an awkward final interview with the director of HR, after she explained that under no circumstances would they allow for flexible schedules; that she'd just actually *extended* the company's in-office hours from nine to six, at minimum; most people stayed until seven in the evening. "Isn't that a mandatory nine-hour workday?" I asked. "Not when you count lunch, it's not," she said, and grinned widely.

I pushed, though I knew I shouldn't if I wanted the job. I argued that having reasonable, thoughtful in-office flexibility was a powerful tool for motivating employees and building trust, and giving your staff a good quality of life was actually better for long-term retention (a stance I still believe in entirely). I was thinking of my future employees, but also myself. It was an hour on the subway each way to this office. If I *had* to be in every day from nine until seven, I would never see my kid. I tried to reason her out of a policy of which she was clearly very proud. I knew if I got the job, I would rarely take a lunch, and I suspected my employees wouldn't either. That wasn't the nature of our business. I said this too. I was raw and on edge. The interview ended abruptly, the HR lady giving a glance at her watch, a closed-mouth grin: "Thanks so much for coming in today." My contact at the company e-mailed me the following week to tell me they'd gone with the other candidate, I was great, et cetera, but the other candidate was a better "cultural" fit. It was my first casualty to work-life balance. Before the baby, I would have worked a hundred in-office hours, but now things had changed.

After this, my level of dissatisfaction as "interim editor in chief" only grew more profound. Instead of focusing on all the exciting new creative freedom I had, freedom I'd wanted for years, I fixated on what I wasn't getting, what I thought I deserved. Instead of looking at the situation as an opportunity, as a chance to audition and win a position I wanted, one that would give me money and stability *and* a relatively flexible office schedule at a company where I was already established, I complained. Instead of inspiring my staff, I gossiped with them. I transferred all my personal anxiety and projected it onto the job—the only thing that brought me satisfaction was grumbling about how incompetent the upper management was, what a shitshow we were in with this *garbage company*. At work, during my downtime, I sought out people I knew I could rope into bitching, who were reliable Negative Nancys, who had BEEF. *Can you believe this shit. This place. Harrumph.* I stomped around the office, self-important and scowling. I was mad-face emoji. If I'd started my career like this, I never would have gotten anywhere.

And this is a common pitfall for many of us as we start to succeed in our careers. Instead of enjoying where we are, we may become disgruntled—a big bag of adult disappointment and accumulated grievances. We zero in on the bad instead of the good. We might be uncomfortable in our new positions, be overly apologetic for and even ashamed of and isolated by our success. We create self-inflicted carrot-and-stick tricks, baiting ourselves to achieve more, climb higher, telling ourselves that it's the *next* promotion that will finally make us feel satisfied and accomplished, the *next* raise that'll generate confidence that we deserve to be in the room, never savoring each hard-won achievement, never fully accepting ourselves.

We may down-talk and make excuses that negate our own good insights, skill, and moments of brilliance: "Oh, well, you know they didn't really give me the title, the job sucks anyway." Or "You know, I mean, a monkey could do this." Or ". . . but I couldn't have done it by myself."*

Now there are obviously legitimate grievances about work that deserve our attention—executives with their heads up their asses, long-term problems at toxic companies that never get resolved that make us feel undervalued. But when these aspects of work become obsessions—even more so as you become senior and the stakes are higher and you have more to lose—it is time to check yourself.

This means examining the situation objectively, taking accountability for your own failings, *and* owning your accomplishments, having a distinct idea of what is in your control and what is not and understanding the role work plays in your life. Without this, without radical introspection, we stagnate, we burn out, our careers stall, we become people others don't want to be around. Constantly laying bare your fear, your anger, your temporary assholery, and identifying what it's all hiding is how you remain open and empathetic. This is how you can authentically inspire people; this is how you gain perspective, fall back in love with what you do, enjoy whatever it is you're doing now, or sort out what you want to do next.

My resentment and anger, the hate I was spewing on that conference call and others like it, had been bubbling under the surface for a long time. My anger was the lockbox where I was

---

* The job is probably fine. A monkey could not do it. And, yes, you could, and you DID.

hiding all of my fear that my success was fragile, that years of hard work could be easily undone by a misstep, that my life was going to collapse, that I was secretly a fraud, that my family would soon live in the subway.

My overthinking, insecurity, and reluctance to lead had not gone away. I was not transformed by higher positions and more esteemed titles; I'd just slapped some glossy management paint over self-consciousness and self-doubt. New motherhood had derailed me, and so had a series of setbacks. I didn't need to pretend those things didn't exist, or that I was infallible and hadn't made mistakes. I just had to forgive myself, regain my footing, and move on.

Sure, the company was chaotic. They should have given me a promotion and a raise if they expected me to do the job, but companies are complex, answers are not always simple, my feelings about this were not their problem. The work of getting over my negative, time-wasting bullshit, of blaming other people and other things for my own unhappiness, fell on me.

One night, after the phone call where I realized I was becoming an asshole, after the baby was asleep, I sat alone and I wrote down everything I loved about my current job and everything I still wanted to do while I was there (lists!). I made a to-do list for that Monday and started thinking about how to get myself excited again. I knew I had a staff of editors and writers I loved, women who were smart and funny and inspiring. So I started there. I scheduled a "big ideas" brainstorm. I helped editors find, write, and edit stories they loved. I went back to what I knew, what made things fun. I focused on serving other people and not myself. For the second time in my career, I shed the business-lady costume and started dressing like myself. I knocked off the corporate lingo and stopped trying to be something I was not. I got curious again and reengaged with my industry, reconnected with professional peers I respected. I typed memos of big, wild ideas and sent them to higher-ups. I looked at the problems in our business and tried to come up with creative solutions. Instead of focusing on what I could not control, I focused on what I could.

In the process I became happier and more fulfilled. Every time I set a goal for myself and met it, I felt more confident that I could do the job. I went back to being a student of my career, I went back to humility, I drove out the fear that was washing over me, that was making me angry and scared. Because I was *doing*. I was active, not passive. I wasn't sitting on the sidelines, bitching. I was proving myself to myself—and to other people too.

I flipped the script, and I became proactive. I didn't have control over what the big tech company would pay me, nor the permanent title I would get. But I could control how I conducted myself every day. I could produce work that made me feel proud. I could help other people get better at their jobs. I could have meaningful interactions in every part of my day. I could stop being an asshole, and I could start to enjoy my work life, such as it was. And when I wasn't in work, I could find time to practice the self-care I so desperately needed so I could be better when I was.

Six months after my boss quit, I secured the big title, the big(ish) pay raise, and the benefits too. Six months later things still weren't perfect, but I was facing them honestly, as myself. Work would never be perfect, I would never be perfect, but I found that I didn't need to be.

CHAPTER 15
Mentorship Matters

I n her book *The Art of Memoir,* Mary Karr says that you should never write about a person you hate. I don't know precisely why she said this, but I can guess. Hate is a superficial snooze. Compassion is complex. Accountability is nuanced. Funny is fun. This is not an ax-to-grind career memoir. I am more filled with gratitude than with loathing for my career; I'd much rather find humor in a situation than hate. In a professional life that has been overwhelmingly filled with luck, goodwill, and kindness, I've encountered only a few insecure bullies, bosses who screamed, slammed doors, called me names—leaders who made the leadership mistakes you make, who were selfish and clumsy, who had little time to teach, let alone "mentor." This happens. It sucks, but it made me stronger. It will make you stronger too.

And I genuinely understand these bosses, especially now that I've been there, walking around in those boss boots. Some days I don't even want to put on clothes, and most days I don't

want to fix my hair, and no days do I want to be on display in
front of dozens of people, telling them what to do. So I don't hate
my terrible bosses. All of them were doing the best they could
at the time of their lives when they were doing it. Some of my
most difficult bosses were managing people and holding down
big jobs while simultaneously enduring some of the most difficult events of their lives—cancer, divorce, the birth of a sick
child, becoming obsolete at the only thing they knew how to do.
Others were simply too inexperienced to do their jobs; they'd
been overpromoted or magically catapulted, their inflated corporate titles meaning as much as being named Chief Kitten.
They failed because they didn't know. And whether this was a
likely outcome or not, I learned a ton from all of them.

However, when I met the best boss I would ever have, a
woman who actually, deeply, preposterously knew how to do
the job of managing while simultaneously kicking ass at the
job of working, it was like discovering a new sense I didn't
know I had, like I was known, like I was professionally home.

My former boss Jessica is unlike any woman I'd met at corporate jobs or any other job. She's smart, fast, unrelenting,
disarming. She's enviably accomplished, has held most of the
impressive-sounding job titles at the most impressive tech companies and earned more-than-she-needs impressive-sounding
degrees. She speaks several languages and has lived and worked
all over the world. She is folksy and charming, a liberal-minded
Kansas girl who spouts Dan Rather–like aphorisms as if she
came up as a ranch hand, and still knows how to artfully throw
the "fucks" around. She also scuba dives, does amateur improv,
and knows everything about bourbon. I'd hate her if I didn't
love her so much. As my boss, I watched her dominate rooms,

eviscerate men trying to give us a bad deal in big partnership negotiations, and then, before walking out, crack a perfectly timed joke and leave the meeting, giving everyone a high five. Her confidence was contagious. She made me *like* business, made it seem fun, helped me stop feeling like an awkward freak and more like the smart, savvy businesswoman she saw in me. I was thirty-seven when I met her—too old for what we think of as the traditional mentor/mentee paradigm—but her influence was worth the wait.

Jessica came into my life as a boss at the big tech company, during a time when, as discussed in the previous chapter (the one you maybe skipped because, gah, I talked about leaking breast milk and New York real estate, zzzzz), I was deflated, angry, and had lost my way. From the day we met, she did the hard work of managing and never backed down from it, zeroing in on my strengths and helping me honestly address my weaknesses. Jessica taught me that your coworkers and the content of your work are important, but it's your boss who really makes you like or hate your job. She taught me that most managers coddle too much. They disempower employees by solving their problems, and in the process don't allow them to learn or grow. She cautioned me not to waste time on underperforming members of my staff. Three months of coaching was enough; anything after that was throwing good effort after bad. She made a profound difference in my life. I gave back to her by working hard and being the best version of myself, not only when I was under her charge but long after I'd moved on.

Jessica was a great mentor to me, yes, and I was lucky to have her, but she wasn't the only one. Over the course of my career, there were many people who supported me, who gave a damn about what happened to me, who called and texted and messaged to make sure everything was OK, even when they were under no obligation to do so, who gave their time generously over coffee and wine and Skype and DM. Who let me sit in their offices and cry, who listened without interruption even when I sounded insane. These were men and women, young and old, people who came into my life briefly along with relationships I've maintained over the long haul. Some of the people who have given me the most insightful career guidance have been my peers; some have been people in different industries, on an entirely different track. But they were all, in their own way, *mentors*, advising and helping me make sound decisions to achieve my goals and advance as far as I could. Mentorship has mattered a great deal in my life, but it didn't come when I thought it would, and it didn't always look the way I thought it should.

And this is important to remember because the idea of getting "mentored" has become formalized and fetishized to a degree that, on top of all the other crap we put on young women, there's now pressure for mentorship to look a certain way, for you to find a kindly fairy godmother/Glinda the Good Witch figure who will dole out bippity-boppity-boo sage advice and cheer for you on the sidelines as you run the marathon of your career. Because of this overemphasis on mentors, I now see young women who feel bad about themselves when they don't have one, adding this to the list of imagined ways they are inferior (1. Can't needlepoint; 2. Apartment/cat/body/bookshelf not Instagram-worthy; 3. I DON'T EVEN HAVE A MENTOR!!!). The fact that we've transformed mentorship—something nurturing that should bring comfort and calm to your life—into a

check on the overachiever checklist is an unnecessary distraction, a new self-defeating obstacle in women's way.

So allow me to assuage your fears and dispel a modern myth:
You don't need a fucking mentor. At least not in the formal
way you imagine you do. You will be completely fine without
one. You need to surround yourself with a network of smart,
supportive people (preferably women) who care about you, who
don't think work is boring, who share your drive and passion,
who are ideally in your profession, or something close. When
you naturally, organically hit it off with someone older or more
experienced who works in your field, whose opinions and work
you respect, whether it be your boss or a coworker or someone
you met on 4chan, you should pick her brain as often as you
can without being rude. You should not call this "picking your
brain," because everyone hates that. You should make your interactions with this person easy and convenient for her, work
around her schedule, be direct, and come prepared for your
meetings with specific questions or concerns. You should not
make this interaction all about you and what you are getting out
of it, but instead think about what you can give back—offer to
buy coffee, bring her a small, inexpensive but thoughtful gift,
follow up with thank-you cards, ask questions about her kids or
kitchen renovation, and try to seem genuinely interested when
she gives boring answers about her kids or kitchen renovation.

Mentoring is not something that will look the same for everyone. You are seeking advice and clarity and support; you
need to be open to getting that from a number of places, over
time. I act as a career guide to nearly every woman who has ever
worked for me, though I don't know that any of them would re-
fer to me as their capital-M Mentor. I help them get new jobs,

negotiate salaries, change careers, rework their résumés, translate awkward LinkedIn messages. I am a forever reference, and each of my former employees uses me in a different way. Some of them text and update me every week; some lose touch for years, until there's a big event and they need critical guidance about what to do next. It's mentoring, I guess, but it's also more basic: I love them, and I genuinely want them to succeed. They are part of my professional tribe. And that's when mentoring works best: when you focus on fostering and maintaining authentic, meaningful professional relationships with people you trust and admire, not worrying about giving those relationships a label, not worrying about fulfilling some arbitrary life #goal. As with everything we've talked about in this book, I urge you not to let your fantasy of what mentoring should look like keep you from experiencing the reality of what it is.

And when it's time for you to start mentoring/acting as a guide/giving advice, make yourself available as often as you can. Listen. Zero in on the other person's needs and don't make it only about your experiences. Be patient. Get off the soapbox. Don't sugarcoat. Be open and honest and unafraid to say what you really think. Stop imagining that you need to be perfect to be worthy of giving advice; you just need to be human and engaged. As women, supporting other women is among the most powerful and long-lasting impacts we can have—expanding far beyond the myopic goals and rewards of a particular job. It's our obligation to help other women, to bring them along with us, to lift each other up, whether we call it mentoring or not. It's vital. It's the least we can do.

CHAPTER 16

Regrets, I Have One

Of course I have more than one regret. I regret trading my Cher doll for a pair of pale yellow Barbie sneakers to a neighbor girl named Sandy when I was seven, a decision I made too excitedly and impulsively because I did not know such a thing existed, and I was tired of Barbie wearing heels, I wanted her to run; a decision I knew immediately after was a mistake.

I regret not making out with that kookily beautiful actor with the crooked teeth from those kookily perfect '90s movies. I regret that when he leaned in to kiss me that night on the balcony, he was wearing a cowboy hat, the brim of which I could not conceive of navigating, so instead I backed away and froze and killed the moment and the moment never returned.

I regret not going to Nicaragua that one time, not going to Russia that other time. I hate the fact that I traveled to Europe for the first time with all of my waitressing savings and a soon-to-be-ex-boyfriend, a man who read aloud from his dream journal at parties and would go on to write a song about me called "Hiroshima." That the only photos I have from that trip are black and white, of me smoking cigarettes I couldn't pronounce and drinking cheap red wine in cheap hotel rooms, while he took moody selfies in front of Jim Morrison's grave at Père Lachaise.

Though I am keenly aware now that I am not a person who should experiment with drugs, I didn't know this in college. In retrospect, it wasn't my smartest idea to try mushrooms that night, or to wear white pants. I regret my part in all the gleeful gossip about that editor who farted* when he got blow jobs, a story I am ashamed to admit I dined out on for years. Generally, my greatest desire would be to go back and erase any hurt or shame I've left in my wake, particularly to my family, clerks at the DMV, and anyone in my high school history class. I regret any time I judged pregnant women or moms before I was pregnant or a mom, because, man, that shit is tough.

However, out of all these many regrets, something good was born—a lesson in negotiation or self-betterment; an improvement in communication style; an epiphany about who I am and how I want to live my life. But the one regret I have that I cannot find redemption in, the one that I am going to tell you about in the hopes that you never do it and never allow it to be done to you, is that time when, for an entire year, at an age when I knew much better, I let a mediocre white man run my life, take away my power, and make me feel small and ashamed.

I was far into the "successful" part of my career when it happened. I had the good title and the good salary. I was twelve

---

* I already regret using the word *fart* in this book.

years into this professional life; I'd hustled and learned—from my own mistakes, from the mistakes of others, from googling the definition of *KPI*. I knew my industry, I'd studied it closely, and I continued to research and pry and push and ask questions, to study the competition and adapt. For the most part I'd kept my nose clean; I'd built a good reputation and a solid professional network of people who I genuinely trusted, respected, and enjoyed. I even had a leadership "style," such as it was. I was tough and no-bullshit, but as a manager I was fair. I liked my job. I was good at it, challenged by it, and fairly compensated for it. This is what I came for.

I'd let men steal my self-confidence and capacity for joy before, of course. The young men of the "He Said" columns in the teen magazines of my youth, the ones who told desperate-to-be-liked girls they had to be something different from what they were—quieter, cleaner, nicer, sexier, scent-ier. The ones who said things like "Too much makeup, such a turnoff!" "I hate it when a girl just orders salad for dinner!"* The sweaty construction worker on my street the summer I was twelve who yelled "She's niiice, but she's got a fat ass!" as I rode my bike up the hill home, a body complex born. The endless dickbag restaurant managers who'd play coy and ask me to spin around in my uniform or pick something up off the floor, who grabbed me sensually around the neck and said I had "hot Italian ears" (whatever the fuck that meant); or the businessmen who, when I balked at having to split their check four ways, suggested that

---

* Later, when I fact-checked at women's magazines, I discovered that almost all of these quotes are made up. Which is even worse, when you think about it—a projection of what women imagine guys wouldn't like about them, essentially girl-on-girl crime.

the math was too hard for me, like I was too foolish and female, too dumb to live, when I was really just doing my job. Later, the men who expected things—sex, mostly—because I was kind or drunk or both. Men who called me a cocktease. Who bought me dinner and said, "Well, you know, when you buy a girl dinner . . ." The men who, when I stood up to them, called me a "bitch," a "cunt," a "cow," a "pig." A "ballbuster." Worse.

I'd dealt with all of those men. Sometimes I stood up for myself; sometimes I walked away. Sometimes I told them to go fuck themselves outright or used that baby voice that is kryptonite to all men and said "Aw, do you feel good about yourself right now? Does that make you feel tough?"

But this man was different.

He was my new boss at a company with lots of men just like him. He was white, but golf-course tan. He owned a Tesla and talked about owning a Tesla and sometimes was on the phone for a long time talking about how someone damaged his Tesla. He had a degree from one Ivy League and another from another Ivy League. I know this because he told me, because he said things like, "When I was at [Ivy League school] . . ." He had a résumé loaded with executive jobs that didn't make sense as jobs, but were really shorthand for "white man gets to push papers/crunch numbers/roll his failure ball up this success hill just because of fancy degrees/whiteness/testicles."

On the first day we met, he invited me, his new female employee, to his office. We spoke of people we had in common, and he told me a story about one such person, a woman at the company where he'd worked before, and how she had shown him her vagina. He did not say vagina, he said her "you know." He reenacted the Sharon Stone *Basic Instinct* scene. *She wasn't wearing panties. I saw her whole, "you know."* He laughed. I turned bright red. I could feel the heat rising from my chest to my neck until my cheeks were burning as if from the deepest sunburn, the ones I'd gotten on the Jersey Shore as a kid, the ones that earned me the nickname "tomato face." *Please don't blush please don't blush don't let this fucking asshole talking about vaginas on his first day see you blush.* I blushed anyway.

I was now the breadwinner of our family. I was a big corporate lady at the big corporation where I worked. After years of deliberation and debate, we'd taken the plunge and moved to a new city. This decision had not come easily—we were leaving everything we knew behind—and it had not come cheaply. Sometimes jobs will "relocate" you, an unthinkable luxury/ perk that includes paying for magical movers to magically pack and transport your stuff, helping you find a place to live, giving you a free place to crash until you do. This job had not; we did not qualify for "relocation." Instead, it took all the money my husband and I had to move to this new city, to get him a better, more consistent-paying job, to live in a better house. The one with the yard. The one that was not an apartment in deep Brooklyn with the flaking-lead-paint windowsills, the no heat, the yelling recluse/madman neighbor downstairs, and the constant thump of a family of six plus a dog upstairs.

Every morning, I left our house at 6:30 to beat traffic and drive seventy-five minutes to make it to my job in this new city. Every morning I missed seeing my not-yet-two-year-old daughter emerge from her bed, downy and perfect, clutching a stuffed bear or a giraffe, gobbling blueberries and toast, saying words she had never said before and would never say in this way again. I was missing this so I could sit in a nondescript fluorescent-lit office while this man talked about vaginas. And sometimes talked about how much he liked getting double-teamed. And how women should wear "fuck-me pumps" to work more.

He made me nervous. Feeling nervous around him made me feel ashamed. When I walked into meetings with groups of other men, he called me "hot pants." He commented on my clothes, my hair, my lipstick, the tones in my voice. He had bad ideas. He took credit for my good ones. He assigned complex, convoluted busywork projects on Friday afternoons and told me to turn them around by Sunday night. When I checked in on Monday to see what he thought, he'd say, "Oh, I never even got around to looking, the weekend just slipped away!"

The company we worked for was in turmoil; rumored layoffs were imminent. When I expressed concern for my job, the man said, "Ooh, I like a woman who's afraid of getting in trouble" and made a "rowr" sound like a domestic cat or a cartoon cat, I wasn't really sure. Then he walked over to where I was sitting and gave me a mini massage, as I tried to turn my shoulders to stone.

Once, when we were on a Very Important Phone Meeting and he was blathering about a problem he did not understand and a solution he could not articulate, I cut him off: "What I think [the man] is trying to say is . . ." I was calm, rational, and succinct. It was simple, really. This is what we should do. Are you with us? Great. Go team.

I left the man's office after the meeting. Less than a minute later, he charged toward my cubicle and ushered me into an empty conference room. He was disappointed and angry, he said. I had cut him off. I'd undermined him in front of other

Very Important People at the company. My behavior was inappropriate. I may have blown the Very Important Deal. I would have to call and apologize. This could never happen again.

He berated me, on and on, until, angry and ashamed, I cried. I told him I was sorry. I told him I was under a lot of pressure. He leaned in for a hug. Then he put his hand on my bare knee, patted it, the most there-there gesture of there-there gestures. He told me he thought it would be OK, that everyone made mistakes. That I shouldn't be so hard on myself.

Before he left the conference room, he told me to pull myself together, call the Very Important People, and make it better. When I called, one Very Important Person said there was no reason to apologize; I was the only thing about that meeting that made any sense.

Here's what I did about the man:

I overthought and obsessed. I schemed and I strategized. I weighed out going to HR and talking to his boss. I wondered if I could get him fired. I fantasized about getting him fired. I got drunk and dreamed up revenge fantasies with my friends. I played it all out in my mind, but I was too scared to act: I thought I would look petty. I thought no one would take me seriously. I thought that the man would get a slap on the wrist, and then he WOULD KNOW how I felt, and then, in subtle, quiet ways, he would make my working life even worse. That I would become ostracized, a pariah at our company, and that, if word got out, I might not be offered opportunities at others. The man knew a lot of people, he reminded me regularly. He was connected in this city. I was not.

Here's what I should have done about the man:

The first time he was inappropriate, I should have looked at him and said, "Talking to me in this way is inappropriate. It should not happen again."

The second time he did it, I should have said, "If you continue to talk to me like this, I will be forced to discuss your behavior with HR."

Then I should have put the conversation in writing, with dates when he said the things he said.

If the behavior persisted, I should have taken my notes and my anecdotes to HR and asked that they correct this behavior and assure me that I would not be punished for addressing inappropriate conduct in the workplace.

Because what I regret the most about that time and those conversations is not hearing about vaginas, obviously, but that I did not defend myself. I was not true to myself. I did not look the man in the eye and tell him to stop. I talk a good game about bravery; I am "intimidating" at work; I would never let what happened to me happen to any of my employees. But when it came time to stand up and protect myself, I failed because I was too afraid, because I didn't think my feelings were important or that anyone would care.

A few years ago, long after the situation with the man had passed, I was on a panel in Austin, discussing "women on the Internet" with two young female editors. We were there for a weekend-long conference, sharing a rented house. At some point we got into an Uber together with a driver, a burly, bearded man, whose behavior was inappropriate and slightly menacing, not so much that you'd jump out of a moving car, but enough that you'd pull out your keys as potential weapons. I don't remember the specifics of what he was saying, but the general vibe was misogynist and bad. I was sitting in the back, on the left; I could see the driver in the mirror. He looked back at me as he ranted. I responded with a little verbal shimmy of pushback without provocation. I was faintly sarcastic, said things like "Oh, you're a funny one." I stood up for us, but not too much. I am a girl of the '70s, with lingering '70s-girl messaging. Don't be a bitch, men might get mad. Men might hurt you. Don't be stupid. Go along, get along. But my companions were younger, and their tolerance for this shit was nonexistent. They assessed the situation. There were more of us than him. "Can you pull over, sir, we'd like to get out here." We were a mile or so from our destination, but it didn't matter. We'd find another car. We were not staying in that one, made to feel that way. This was for sure.

I am a smart, independent woman. I'm a feminist. But I had not thought of getting out of the car that day; I had not thought of confronting the man who harassed me that year. There was still a lingering part of me, one you'd never see on social media, that felt it was my duty to please, that deep down thought the behavior wasn't so terrible, that my discomfort was the problem, that maybe I deserved it all because I was fundamentally a bitch, a "ballbuster," bad. That because this man liked Armani-suit-clad ladies with blowouts, he could not possibly be intimidated by or want to fuck weirdo me, and so maybe this was all in my head.

But what I realized that day in Austin and have continued to learn since is that it is not wishy-washy or insecure to prevent this from happening and to change the way some men behave in workplaces. It's strong and extreme. It requires all of us to be tougher than we think we are. It's zero tolerance of sexual intimidation and gender-based power games, no matter how slight. I urge you to institute this policy—even when it's scary, even when you feel doubtful, or afraid that you won't be liked. I urge you not to play along, not to act like it's cool, like it's cute ever, not when you're twenty-three and not when you're fifty-three. To never regret not standing up for yourself, not ever again. I urge you because enough already: women deserve to be treated equally and respectfully at workplaces and other places, now and forever, the end.

CHAPTER 17

Get a Life

I n late summer of 2015, I was stalking a person on social media with whom I compete in my mind. This person and I are casual friends, and I actually like her very much, but she always seems one step ahead of me professionally and personally, and because of this and because I am a competitive person, I feel the jealousy burn when I look at her. I consider us rivals, even though we are not actually rivals, and I always dislike her just a bit, a fact that makes me feel cringey and small, as it should. So this night when I was stalking, this person had posted a picture of herself with a group of people and she was laughing. Like a full-body, unselfconscious laugh, the kind that shows all your teeth and squinty eyes and even a double chin. The kind you don't usually see on social media because it is not pretty and it is not perfect and is instead real. I studied and studied and studied this picture. I clicked the geotag to see where the event was, to feel it more viscerally. I clicked on other people who were tagged, even though I did not know them. I was a detective gathering and piecing together the evidence, I was Nancy Drew trying to solve the case: Why was this woman so happy?

Then, because jealousy always brings up the most real things in me, I asked a second question: Why was I not? I could not remember the last time I'd felt truly happy. I could not remember a time when I was laughing like that woman was laughing. I could not remember being present enough in a particular situation when I was connecting with other people that I could access that kind of joy. I had "everything"—I was a mother to an outrageously smart and wonderful daughter, I was a partner to a man I adored and respected, I had reached the highest position I could in an amazing job I loved—but I was also utterly stressed and overstretched, frantic throughout every aspect of my day, playing and winning the Whack-a-Mole game of my life but enjoying very little of it.

I'd spent the past two years as the editor in chief and vice president of content at a start-up website for young women, a brand that I loved and believed in and gave all my creative and strategic energy to transform and grow. I was working seven days a week—no nonworking vacations, no self-care breaks. Like most start-ups, our entire staff was barreling through at warp speeds, growing the business as big and as fast as we could with the fewest resources possible, headed toward charmed-exit* success or a brand-purgatory abyss, not knowing which one we'd get until we were there. Blink, and we'd miss the opportunity of a lifetime. Blink, and we were irrelevant and it all went away. It was exhilarating, it was exhausting, it was addicting, and it consumed everything I had.

In my "downtime," I felt crippled, overloaded, and pulled in too many directions, all Goldie Hawn, monosyllabic in the

---

* Sale to a big company.

tank in *Overboard*: "Buh-buh-buh-buh-buh." It was as if I'd re-ordered my brain to only think about work and only talk about work, and when it wasn't doing those things, it short-circuited. I woke up in the middle of the night and made to-do lists. I woke up in the middle of the night and answered e-mails. Desperate to catch up, I made my workdays longer and longer, starting earlier and earlier. In an attempt to be more efficient, I logged on to my computer from home at 4:30 a.m., putting in three hours of work before most people were even awake. When I came home from work at 7:00 p.m., after dinner, after cleanup and playtime, after asking clumsy kid questions and listening to adorable kid non-answers, I put my daughter in a bath and kept her there longer than she naturally needed to get clean so I could answer e-mails while she pruned. Because they couldn't wait an hour until bedtime. Because I needed a work check in between bath and bed.

All of this had taken a toll on me physically and emotionally. I was distracted and edgy with everyone in my family. I zoned out in important personal conversations. My second marriage was in a fragile state at best, in serious fucking trouble at worst. And then my kid started having problems.

Psychics Say the Darnedest Things

The office of the start-up I worked for was an unconventional girlie dream—all flowers and puppy art, positive aphorisms, glitter-strewn desks, sparkly fabric panes, tiaras, carved bowls overflowing with candy, the detritus from elaborate nail art scattered about. A life-size skeleton constantly moved around the space, dressed up and positioned in peculiar ways by the staff, according to the season—an ongoing inside visual joke, an homage to the daily delight and creative randomness that inspired the room. We brought in boxes of pastel-hued macarons, we admired each other's clog sandals, our soundtrack was Beyoncé-dominant. The bookshelves were bursting with graphic novels, self-help books, the complete collections of both Sweet Valley High and Harry Potter; the midcentury sofas and chairs were strewn with furry pillows and cozy lap blankets; the lighting was warm and dim. In one corner, you'd find a signed headshot of the *Perfect Strangers* cast; in another, a rose-quartz crystal larger than a Duraflame log, thicker than a thigh. Meditation practice was heralded; sage smoke was regularly deployed. I'd engage in a half-hour conversation about the pros of an Ayurvedic-based cleanse and then return to my desk and edit essays about topics ranging from intersectional feminism to Mercury Retrograde to *Gilmore Girls*.

On the day that we were offered the services of a major pop star's psychic, I signed up. It seemed a natural extension of the job.

It took a month to get an appointment with the pop star's psychic. We e-mailed back and forth to find a convenient time. I felt annoyed by this, like she should somehow know what time would work. In the weeks before we spoke, I was skeptical about the entire thing. I used our upcoming session as a punchline to stories told at backyard barbeques about how strange my life had become. When the day of the appointment finally arrived, I called the psychic from my office, notebook open, pen in hand. When I picked up the phone and dialed, I was surprised to find I was nervous.

The psychic told me I should stop eating tomatoes. The psychic told me I should see my mother-in-law more. The psychic was a woman with a man's name and a throaty voice who sounded bored and distracted through the receiver, like she might fall asleep midsentence, like this was all so mundane. She told me things that could apply to me but also to anyone. She "saw" things. She saw that my husband and I fought over laundry. She saw that we had a pet. She thought my daughter's bedroom was not set up correctly. She said my daughter needed a desk. She told me that she did not see me having another baby, but she saw a "very special baby soul" who would come into my life in the next year.

Here are three other things she saw:

"In the next six months you will not be doing what you do now professionally."

"In the next three months, I see you signing papers. You will sign at least two sets of papers coinciding with two very big deals."

"In the next two months your daughter is going to need you more than she's ever needed you before."

We hung up. I called my husband, and we laughed. I said we should hire someone to do our laundry. I said maybe we needed to visit his mom. I sent a check to the woman with the man's name for the fee upon which we'd agreed. I did not purchase the spirit cards she recommended, or the pendulum. I did not stop eating tomatoes.

Six months later, everything the psychic said had come true.

What Dreams May Come

Here is a secret. I always wanted to write a book. For a long time, all through college (both times) and my late twenties, I kept this desire hidden. It felt silly and pompous to admit it, so everyone's-got-a-novel-in-'em cliché, so pretentious in that liberal-arts-college-boy way, endlessly prattling about short-story collections or books of poetry that would never come to light and, if they did, were vapid and trite and not very good.

For a long time after that, while I was living in New York, years before my very Los Angeles conversation with the psychic, I talked about wanting to write a book *all the time*. It was all I talked about to anyone, in bars and coffee shops, on dates with new men and on the phone with old friends, in the bathroom to my roommate, in the mirror to myself. And then I tried to write a book. I got an agent and I wrote a proposal and the proposal was sent to a bunch of book editors and no one liked it. It tanked. No one wanted to pay me to write a book. After we received the final rejection, I drank a million drinks and ugly-cried in public and made my agent at the time—a person who is no longer my agent—visibly uncomfortable, a cringe-face meme. I called my then boyfriend, now husband, to meet and take me home, col-lapsing into his body upon arrival, a sloppy bundle of failure and sads. The next day, while swallowing Advil and shame, I decided that though I had many skills and had achieved many things, writing a book probably wasn't going to be one of them. Still, after this, because I am not a quitter, I half-assedly wrote two more book proposals, one on female friendship and one on the seasons, both so bad that the agent who is no longer my agent stopped answering my calls. My fear that I didn't have the talent nor the good ideas to take on a project like this was now borne out as resoundingly true. I'd tried and I'd failed, and it was time to brush myself off and move on.

But the dream to write a book did not brush off; it stuck around. It was a subtle irritation, nagging at me like the tiniest splinter under the smallest nail, a wincing discomfort anytime I thought about it and pressure was applied. It stayed with me as I sat on very professional business panels and spoke into microphones saying very professional business words, as I gave speeches on stages about digital media trends while wearing tweedy skirts and too much gold. It did not go away when I appeared twitchy on live TV in front of Hoda and Kathy Lee, as the man next to me talked about dating trends and boobs, when I sat in an oversize chair across from Anderson Cooper to explain what was "hot" now, nor when I was interviewed for a newspaper to discuss my "style." There was something else I wanted to do, something creative and naked and risky, which went beyond big leadership and big titles, media appearances and fancy events, which transcended any and all external measures of success. There was something I still craved professionally, something personal and authentic and deep, something that scared me more than anything else. It was a dream I'd long had but never fulfilled, and if I didn't pursue it, I knew it was going to gnaw at me—if not forever, for a very long time.

I don't know how I got up the nerve after that call with the psychic to competently learn and complete all the dance steps required in the selling-a-book dance*. I don't know how I did

---

* Having a spectacular agent helped.

this while working a seven-day-a-week job and, especially, while tending to the needs of my precocious, demanding five-year-old, who, as the psychic had foretold, suddenly required acute guidance and emotional care. Just weeks after the psychic reading I'm still not sure I believe in, my daughter's unconventional behavior had become a concern, one that demanded a great deal of time, research, and attention, involved multiple weekly meetings with administrators and teachers, drop-of-the-hat summons to school to pick her up early/bring different shoes/referee a fight about turtles—hours of hassle and worry and discussions about what was *actually* wrong, if there was actually *anything* wrong. Since kindergarten started, my daughter had come home most nights and cried. She was anxious, couldn't make friends, was disciplined frequently by teachers while all the kids stared. She felt left out and odd. After she went to bed at night, I cried too. Her experience triggered something in my deepest misfit core.

In the midst of watching the weird girl I loved more than anything struggle to find her place in the world for the first time, a struggle that I profoundly understood, I wrote a book proposal about being a weird woman in the adult working world; about how, for some of us, feeling awkward and fighting to find our place never goes away; about how it doesn't have to.

Two months after I talked to the psychic, I sold this book.

A month after that, the start-up where I was working was acquired.

Everything was happening as it should.

I'm OK, You're OK

One night after coming home from work late, while my husband was out at a work event and my daughter was yelling at me for not participating in Mad Libs and the cat had barfed on the floor and the TV volume was deafeningly loud and dinner was burning and everything was a scene from a '90s sitcom about the colorful-hilarious-hapless chaos of raising a child, an old friend called. I updated her on all of my too-good-to-be-true news: I sold a book! I helped sell a company! I'd been offered a big position and a generous contract to stay on at the new super company, one that involved lots of executive responsibility and travel! I'd write the book at night and on weekends! Life was all going to be GRAND! This friend knows me well, but perhaps more important, she is a human with working ears. After assessing the panic in my voice and the mayhem on my side of the phone, she said, "I hate to say this, but I don't think you're going to be able to do all of the things you want to do here. At least not well. You can't be a super-present mom, work an intense new job, and write a book all at the same time. You don't get all three. You have to pick two."

For nearly two decades, I'd approached my career with a kind of masochism: the more it hurt, the better I was doing. I wore "workaholic" and "careerist" like badges of pride. I loved working, and I'd poured a great deal of myself into thinking about, strategizing for, and expanding my professional life. My hard work had paid off in ways I'd hadn't even imagined possible—beyond just money and stability, each career hurdle validated my ability and increased my confidence, each promotion and new job helped me shape who I was and could be. But I knew rationally I'd reached an impasse. I knew my approach to office life had worn me down, that I was burned out, that my current position did not give me the thrill it once had. I did not want to be the kind of manager who hangs on for too long and phones it in. I didn't want to phone it in with my kid either, not at this moment, not for this year. To move forward successfully, I was going to have to step back. To fulfill a new dream, I was going to have to change course.

Still, the idea of quitting my job horrified me. I couldn't remember myself without a job-job. I was afraid that without the structure and the inherent responsibilities of a big position, I'd regress and fall apart. My unchecked neurosis and residual self-doubt would take over; I'd sit around drinking flat prosecco too early and out of the bottle, stuffing my mouth with stale Bugles while watching *The View*. What if I took the risk and failed? I did not want to give up my financial safety net. I could find a way to make it all work.

I called my dad, the hardest worker I know, a person who, now in his sixties, still puts in ten-hour days at work, on his feet, in basically a walk-in refrigerator. His mantra for me around work has always been simple, practical, stability-first: work hard, stop whining, put food on your table and a roof over your head. When I explained my situation, I expected him to tell me to suck it up, that it wouldn't be so bad, that it would be over before I knew it. Instead he said: "You've been given a shot with this book, an opportunity to do something you really want to do. Most people don't get that. Don't half-ass it. Take the shot."

And so I did. I took the shot.

I picked two.

The grass is not greener on this side, it's just different. I've learned that picking my daughter up from school in the afternoon makes me happier than just about anything, and I'm grateful for every day I get to do it. I've learned that I am not a domestic queen, and having more free time did not inspire an addiction to exercise, as I'd hoped. I've learned that the best time to go to the grocery store is 9:45 a.m. on a Monday, and play dates are hell whether you are stay-at-home or not. I sometimes miss the challenge of office work and collaborating with other humans; I often miss the structure that gets me up and away from my brain. I still can't believe that the only e-mails I get are from Groupon. It's been odd and strange to not be accountable to anything except my family and myself and this book.*

But none of this matters as much as this: taking a risk and a step back, facing myself down, examining my unhappiness instead of hiding it away, asking myself difficult questions and coming up with and acting on true answers—it did not make me irrelevant, as I'd feared. It made me more myself—happier, lighter, more creative, engaged, and present, by any measure, better prepared for whatever comes next. I spent so many years of my life tense and afraid, worried that if I ever got off the ride, they'd never let me back on. Worried that if I didn't do it all just right, they'd kick me off. In my fear, I failed to see the alternative, to recognize that there wasn't just one ride but an entire carnival around me.

---

* Though, by the time you read this, I'll most likely be standing at my next stand-up desk, eating all the free office snacks, and raining my particular brand of smarts/weirdness/hustle onto my next unsuspecting job.

Your story will be different from mine. It may not follow my structure; it may not involve a traditional path of any kind. You may not zero in on one career and follow it for years; you may be multiplatform and multidimensional and find multiple, wonderful challenges and ways to succeed at being you. But whatever you are and whatever you choose, what I want for you is this: I want you to dream gigantically, even when it feels ridiculous, even when you're scared, even when you feel too weird and anxious and raw to keep going. I want you to be relentless in pursuing those dreams, to never give up on them or yourself, to live your life as a hedge against future regret. I want you to work on something you love until you collapse in exhaustion, satisfied. I want you feel the exhilaration and self-pride of every big and small success, of your power and ownership over your professional destiny, over the fact that you can do anything, and you should.

And in this time when you are dreaming and pursuing and fulfilling, in this time when you are proving yourself to the world, but mainly, most importantly, to yourself, you may be an ambitious, competitive, career-hungry animal. You may never stop thinking about work; you may put in too many hours and sleep with your phone and stalk the trends of your business the way some people follow sports. All of this is cool. Until one day maybe it's not.

Don't work so much that you lose yourself. Find love in your life. Pet all the puppies. Go to the beach. If you hate the beach, climb up a mountain. If you have a good relationship with your family, maintain it. Don't miss your best friend's wedding or your dad's retirement party because of a job. Don't miss things that are important to you—whatever they are—because some unreasonable boss tells you to. If you feel like you're going too fast, if you've lost yourself in dogged determination, in the upward movement of your career, slow down.

The meaning of success is elastic, adjustable. Yours cannot be quantified by anyone but you; it's whatever feels right to you at the time when it's happening. As women, we've fought to be anything we want, and if what we want is to work a hundred hours a week OR stay at home and nap with babies OR take a break from office life and sit on our fannies writing our first book while mainlining LaCroix—and we can still put a roof over our heads (rented or not) and food on our tables (folding or gold-plated)—it's all OK.

Because here is what success and "making it" really looks like: it's not about money, though that's a nice perk. It's not about superimpressive titles, though this will make you feel good and help assuage your superficial fears.

What "making it" really means is this: it means loving what you do and being true to who you are; it means working hard but setting boundaries for that work so you can live your life too. It means being compassionate to yourself and others along the way. Once you make it, success means giving back to other people. It means showing up and being great every day, not acting like a jerk, not endorsing jerks, and trying, somehow, to enjoy the ride.

Success for us misfits means remembering over and over: you are not too weird or fucked up for this world. You don't have to accept a life where you're simply punching a clock. You can shape-shift and transform, again and again. You can be courageous and curious, challenged and sanguine. You can make the world come to you. Not despite being weird, but because of it.

Acknowledgments

eird in a World That's Not would not have been possible without my friend and agent Byrd Leavell, who understood this book right away and gracefully shepherded me, and it, over the finish line. It wouldn't exist without my editors, Hollis Heimbouch and Stephanie Hitchcock, whose sharp, no-nonsense guidance helped me deliver more than I thought I could.

I am indebted to the smart women who took time to read this book early, who gave thoughtful feedback and made it infinitely better: Piper Weiss, Gina Mei, Taylor Trudon, Sarah McColl, Kayleigh Roberts, Kristen Lisanti.

For the #boss women who taught me to be a better one: Sara Nelson, Jessica Jensen, Annette Cardwell, Lori Bongiorno, Kim France. And for David Carr, who gave a damn.

Writing a book is a lonely enterprise; it can make you strange. I am forever grateful for the support of the following humans while I was writing this one: Rumaan Alam, Clayton Doyle, Matt and Kristy Alper, Claire Girolo, Liz Flahive, Jeff Cox. My family—Joe, Lynn, Nicolas, Michele—a gaggle of beautiful weirdos. My daughter, Charlotte Jane Pappademas, who makes everything better. To feel known and loved for who you truly are is the best we can hope for in this life. I am lucky beyond measure for my brilliant husband, Alex Pappademas, who knows that I am but an awkward wolf in lady's clothes and who loves me because of it.

About the Author

JENNIFER ROMOLINI is the chief content officer of Shondaland .com, a website founded by Shonda Rhimes. She was previously the editor in chief of HelloGiggles and Yahoo Shine, and the deputy editor of *Lucky* magazine. Her writing has appeared in the *New York Times* and *Lenny Letter*. She lives in Los Angeles.